T0149410

A Jar Full of
Fireflies

SHARON SPENCE

BALBOA.
PRESS
A DIVISION OF HAY HOUSE

Cover Credits: Julie Perkins, Artist. Robyn Burnett and Peter Hoare photography

Balboa Press books may be ordered through booksellers or by contacting:

Balboa Press
A Division of Hay House
1663 Liberty Drive
Bloomington, IN 47403
www.balboapress.com.au
1 (877) 407-4847

Print information available on the last page.

ISBN: 978-1-5043-0687-4 (sc)
ISBN: 978-1-5043-0688-1 (e)

Balboa Press rev. date: 02/23/2017

Introduction

How do we find the wealth of self-help information that's available when we have no money? How do we access it when we are socially controlled or financially isolated? What if we have an abusive partner who monitors every Internet search or checks our phones?

What if simply trying to hold life together and make it through another day takes everything we have? How can we set off on the road to self-discovery, never mind find the road to self-improvement?

When the pain of the present prevents us from unearthing and releasing the pain from the past, we get stuck. We become caught in the slipstream of life. Years pass by, and the fear of facing the truth of just how we arrived at this spot, never mind how we can move on, becomes even harder to contemplate … and so we remain firmly stuck.

These are the difficulties I faced, and more, before I could escape from a limiting life in which I had experienced death, rejection, and loveless abusive relationships.

Life was normal until, at the age of thirteen, my father died suddenly of a massive heart attack. He was aged forty. My world was thrown into a chaotic mess. Unable to comprehend the impact of his death and unsupported in my grief, my emotions were supressed to the point that I simply travelled through life like a puppet, dancing to every tune but my own for fear of upsetting, or being upset. Desperate for love and understanding, I fell into a long-term relationship that was a rollercoaster of abuse and torment. I had even become resigned to the prospect of an early death as a direct result of the stress I was living with. Divorce, a loveless relationship and a failed engagement were still to follow.

My journey back to wholeness did not begin with jumping into a self-discovery course, nor did it begin with life coaching or therapy. The prospect of dealing with any of that was simply too much to consider. Instead, my journey began with just one sentence: "twenty-eight days to change my life." I began collecting words and phrases that simply resonated with me. I see them now as being sacred sparks from the Divine. The words spoke to me in ways no one ever had. Writing and playing with words offered me a safe means to express my deeply suppressed emotions. For the first time, I was communicating with my inner self, and I found it deeply therapeutic. I had always found it very difficult to articulate my feelings, never mind communicate them with anyone. I had been abused for speaking up and had become conditioned to not speaking, not being heard, and not being valued. I found that for the first time in my life, words just flew from my head and heart onto paper.

One page of words offered me insight. Two pages pointed to new ways of thinking. Three pages fuelled me on, until I slowly began to see my story woven there on the page. I built a map of my life, unravelling deep pain and limiting beliefs. Beautiful words helped me dream of the new life I desired.

Slowly, those beautiful words became thoughts and actions. New beliefs were formed, and the light from my soul just continued to grow. It was the start of an incredible, gentle journey in which I found love, happiness, and freedom. I found courage to face my grief, unravelled myself from my tangled past, let go of loveless relationships, and bloomed. My life filled with so much love and understanding that I formed new theories about living, death and dying, so much so, that I went on to work as a volunteer with the terminally ill in their last few weeks of life. I travelled full circle and found freedom and joy at a level I can only remember experiencing as a child. All it took to get me started was a gentle spark. All it took to keep me going was the ability to dream, visualise, and listen to my soul. The universe took care of everything else.

Words can take us many places and offer great truths when they are written from the heart, touch our soul, and spark the sacred within. Words were my saving grace. They taught me to turn sorrow into valuable life lessons, find comfort in the simplest of joys and ultimately, find myself again.

When standing in a place of darkness,
all too often the prospect of stepping boldly into the glaring light
is too much to bear.
Consider instead, a gentle soul journey in search of fireflies.
Fireflies offer you their gift of illumination.
They find you in the darkness, and willingly,
they enter your empty jar of hope.
Slowly, your jar begins to fill with beautiful light.
Soft light.
Nurturing light.
Then one day, you realise your jar is full.
The darkness has gone.
Your life has become illuminated in the most magical way possible,
your heart and soul enlightened once again.

These are my fireflies.
My gifts of illumination to you.
May they guide you home to wholeness,
where your light never fades.

To the very special women who have graced my life with love and wisdom,
thank you for helping me find freedom. To my darling daughter, thank
you for your strength, compassion, and unwavering love. To my beautiful
son, thank you for your bountiful, unconditional love and support.
Neither time nor distance nor death will ever erase
the memories of such beautiful people.
I love you all.

To my darling father,
thank you for your guiding spirit and infinite love.
You are always by my side and forever in my heart.
Can't wait to see you again.

A Sacred Blessing as You Begin Your Journey

May you have faith that your future is safe.

May you accept that your every choice has brought you to this point in your journey.

May you find security in the knowledge there is no beginning and no end in this universe.

For this will bring you the peace you desire.

May you find self-acceptance.

May you know you are pure love.

May you allow passion into your life.

May you grant yourself permission to dance through this life.

For this will bring you the dreams you desire.

May you see only the reflection of your beautiful inner light.

May you allow yourself to feel pure emotion.

May you see the vast abundance that is already all around you.

For this will bring you the strength you desire.

May you release resentment from your heart and find restful peace.

May you find clarity and strength to make positive change.

May you be open to your heart's desires and

answer the calling of your soul.

For this will bring you the freedom you desire.

May you may be blessed with love and grace on your journey in search of fireflies.

Awaken

Feel the stirring of your soul.
What does it seek?
Listen carefully.
It is calling you to take action.
Close your ears to words of doubt.
Let your eyes see only truth.
Allow your courage to roar.

Every day, I would drive alongside a field where an abandoned, crumbling old cottage sat surrounded by a mass of dark, gnarly trees. It reminded me of a scene from a horror movie.

I wondered how the cottage would have looked in its youth. I tried to imagine the stonework in perfect order, creamy in colour and clean. I would see the tin roof and wooden windows in order, keeping the elements at bay. I imagined a long driveway leading to the place someone had once called home. However, the trees would always cut short my vision. They stood out for all the wrong reasons, and I wondered for a long time why they hadn't been cut down. That was before I witnessed their incredible springtime transformation for the first time.

Every one of the dead, dark, gnarly trees suddenly burst into life with a magical display of the most beautiful, delicate pink blossoms. Not one failed to bloom. The field was instantly transformed with a mammoth flurry of pink blossom petals.

All it took was the right conditions for the trees to bloom. They had sat there dormant, innocently and patiently waiting for spring. Did they realise their dead look could have been enough for them to be cut down and their beauty lost forever?

Sometimes, we too have to retreat into a dormant state, where we patiently await our own spring to come around in order for us to bloom again. Just like the trees, being in this dormant state preserves and protects our inner sanctum from the harsh life elements that surround us. It is a necessary function in order to survive while we wait for the return of the right conditions that will see us bloom again. It is a natural process to go through and one that all too often we are denied, due to demands placed upon us to always be and look "happy".

Nature has many lessons to teach us: lessons of survival, of restraint, and of unbridled regenerative power.

If we feel as if we are in a current state of dormancy, or heading there, a walk in nature will quickly nurture our soul. A walk among a pine forest after a rain storm, or along a windswept beach, will quickly remind us of our own fragility and delicacy. It will also remind us of the innate strength and regenerative ability that lies within. It will show us the yin and yang of life, which we are, of course, a great part of. It will teach us that dormancy is a natural survival tactic and a successful one.

If you are experiencing "dead wood" syndrome at the moment, take time and be gentle with yourself. Let nature remind you how to achieve balance and harmony through rest and renewal and connection with the elements.

When the time is right, you will bloom magnificently and shower the world in your very own cotton candy-coloured blossoms.

Sacred Renewal Ritual

Awaken to Your Dreams

It is time to plant dreams.
It is time to nourish oneself with passion and joy.
It is time for wishes to be fulfilled.

This ritual will aid in the manifestation of your heart's desires.

Creating Sacred Space

Create a sacred space with red flowers for passion. Add four candles to represent fire and rebirth. Their light represents the very energy you wish to attune to. As you light each candle, call upon the elemental forces of the earth to activate your ritual:

- north: the element of earth for strength
- east: the element of air to carry away your troubles
- south: the element of fire for purification
- west: the element of water for cleansing

Adding fragrance in an oil burner or to a bowl of water heightens the power of the ritual.

You may use patchouli oil, which is a stimulating aphrodisiac, or sandalwood to evoke a meditative atmosphere. Whatever you choose will be right for you.

As you pour droplets of the essential oil, give thanks to their over soul in acknowledgement of their gift to you. Sit quietly and take a few deep breaths. Look at the beautiful sacred space you have created. Listen to the sounds around you. Breathe in the fragrance you have chosen, the scent of the flowers, and the warm molten candle wax. Be aware of whatever taste you have in your mouth. Be aware of the touch of the clothes on your skin. Be grateful for the gift of your senses.

Let your focus fall on your breath. With each in breath, welcome in peace. With each out breath, send out love.

Feeling safe and relaxed, let your attention go to the centre of your heart. You see the glow of a soft green light. Focus on the light and see it become more intense. The green becomes deeper in colour and intensity. The middle of your chest is glowing in iridescent light.

Soon you notice the light from your heart centre has completely surrounded you.

The entire room is now glowing with emerald magnificence.
In front of you, a green door appears.
It is an old door made from ancient timbers.
Step towards the door and pull on the solid latch.
As you open the door, you see a meadow before you.
It stretches as far as your eyes can see.
Step through the door.
You have nothing to fear.

Feel your feet plant themselves firmly on the ground as you pass through the door into the meadow.
Feel lush green grass under your bare feet.
You have entered a sacred meadow.
Wriggle your toes; feel the softness of the grass underfoot.
Take a deep breath and devour the scent of fresh green grass.

The meadow is covered in beautiful, delicate flowers of every colour of the rainbow.
In one quick moment, wild flowers surround you.
They reach out to touch you as you pass.
They beckon you to lay down and spend time in their loving embrace.
Their easy motion and sweet perfume lull you into a state of deep peace.
Lay down for a moment.

Let the meadow flowers wrap around you like a beautiful blanket, keeping you warm and safe.

Looking into the sky, you see a butterfly gently fluttering towards you.
Its wings are vivid blue.
It lands upon your nose to rest.

Smile at this blissful encounter with such an innocent creature.
Notice there is something attached to this butterfly.

It is a tiny ribbon of a colour that only you know.
On the ribbon, you see written in tiny words
"Tell me your wish".

You whisper your innermost heart's desire to the butterfly
and watch as your spoken words appear on the ribbon, as if by magic.
They are written in delicate silver thread.
Your butterfly takes flight and heads for a nearby tree.
As you look closer at the tree, you see it is covered in ribbons of every colour,
embellished with silver threads.
Your ribbon has found its place on the tree.

This is the sacred desire tree, tended by the guardians of the meadow for
those of pure heart.
It is only as the delicate flowers unfurl around you
that you notice butterflies in their millions, flying across the meadow to
the tree and then back into the clear blue sky.

Feel blessed for this remarkable encounter.
Give thanks to the butterfly, the ancient tree, the beautiful flowers, and the
soft green grass.
Inhale the scent of the sacred meadow one last time.
Then step back through the ancient door.
You are home.

Relax in your sacred space for as long as you feel necessary.
When you are ready, give thanks to Mother Earth and the elements for
their life force.

You may wish to write down your desires and gently tie them to a favourite
tree with coloured ribbons. Or you may simply record them in your
affirmation journal.

Discovery

Catch the wind.
Feel the sun.
Hear the ocean calling.
Surround yourself with things
that tell a beautiful story.

Have you ever arrived at a destination, only to think, *I don't remember getting here?* As we go through the motions of our day, we are generally on autopilot. We move through throngs of people, looking, but not really seeing. We hear them, but we are not listening. We respond automatically, without thinking.

Our heads are so full of thoughts of things we desire or need in order to get to where we want to be in life.

We move through life, searching for things to acquire because of what we feel they do for us and how much better we perceive we will feel when we have them. We are glitter seekers. But what are we missing if we focus only on these things, which we expect will add some glitter to our lives?

I regularly walked along the same path from my home, which ran parallel to a busy main road. The footpath was in pretty bad shape, and ultimately, I became uninspired with this route. It was not pleasant to the eye, and my mind was always full of chatter; I fell out of rhythm with walking altogether.

One day, I decided to walk the route again, but I made a commitment to myself to look at it with fresh eyes. I decided I would not look at the condition of the road or footpath, or the number of cars and homes along the way. Instead, I would look for things that I probably passed by a million times and never took notice of, and I would cease my mind chatter by running a commentary in my head.

I discovered an olive tree at the start of the footpath, not too far from my home. It was in full bloom, with tiny olives on every branch. Tiny white, pink, lilac, and ruby flowers dotted the footpath with beautiful bursts of colour. Fat bees sat upon the tiniest of flowers, bending in the breeze. Gorgeous bamboo shoots lined the creek bed. With greatness and strength, the mature shoots protected the fresh young green shoots as they flourished and found their way upwards towards the sky. At a glade, a beautiful kangaroo and her joey stood together in the long grass. How many times had I missed these things? Tiny balls of flowers and tiny white trumpet flowers grew in places where it seemed impossible ... and then I reached the ocean at the end of the footpath. It never ceases to take my breath away.

The colours are even more beautiful when the sand mixes with the whitewash, and the sky blends smoothly into the horizon. I realised just how blessed I was to be there in the moment, to see such beauty, to hear the ocean, to feel the wind on my face and the sand beneath my feet. The scent of the seawater was incredible, as was the unexpected nudge from the wet nose of a beautiful dog that stopped to say hello. I couldn't resist saying hello right back.

From my one conscious decision to approach something differently, I had a completely new and amazing experience. It made me think. What if I could go back to the day before and instead of moving through it on autopilot, I had the chance to relive it consciously? Would I see just how many opportunities I missed, where I could have thanked someone, smiled, touched them with kindness, looked them in the eye as they spoke to me? Would I see how many times I missed the opportunity to help another? What beauty had I missed by being so distracted?

I had become so aware of the stunning amount of abundance that surrounded me, just by looking at one part of one day in a different way. I saw the solid gold that is underneath all of the glittery distractions we are so mesmerised by, and from that moment on, I chose consciousness.

A Divine Gift for You

The universe sends love to soothe your cares.
Like golden snowflakes, love falls upon you.
As each snowflake settles upon your skin,
your heart beats faster in recognition of something wonderful.
Your skin is aglow as your body and soul bathe in the
endless love that is being showered upon you.
It fills you up.
It nourishes you.
Allow universal love to light any darkness
so as each new day dawns,
you awaken with a heart full of hope,
joy, and happiness,
and above all,
love.

Acceptance

Close your eyes and breathe.
Everything is going to be just fine.
You are exactly where you need to be right now.
Surrender and let in peace.

If you saw the movie *Willy Wonka and the Chocolate Factory*, you may remember Veruca Salt. Veruca was one of the lucky children who found a golden ticket and entered the magical chocolate factory. Veruca was famous for her "I want it *now*." tantrums. She was a demanding child, to the say the least.

The movie was released in 1971, when life was considerably calmer. Today, we live in a world where everything is delivered in an instant and expected in an instant. Goods, services, work demands, home demands, and replies to texts, emails, Facebook messages, tweets … they never stop. The list is endless, and the pressure to produce and receive on demand is increasing.

All of us want something: success; peace; a new job; a new partner; to be slimmer, fitter, healthier, wealthier; to go on vacation; to get back from vacation; to catch up with everything we've fallen behind with; for it to be Friday again when it's only Monday morning; to win the lottery and never have to work again. Do we want to wait for any of that? No, we want it now. Admit it: We all have a piece of Veruca Salt in us.

Okay, so we may not scream out our demands like Veruca, but we sure do internalise them. So, is it okay to internalise rather than verbalise our demands? If nobody hears our demands, is that okay? On the face of it, yes, but someone always hears our demands: We do. Our soul hears them, and the universe hears them.

The universe listens to all of our demands: every single one of them. To make things worse, we make double-sided demands such as, "I really want the job, but I know I won't get it." or "I want to win the lottery, but I never will." Sound familiar? Just what is the universe meant to do with double-sided demands like that?

When we send out double-sided demands to the universe (vocally or internally), we remain in a state of stasis. We may ultimately get what we want, but it will not come to us easily.

Instead of sending out double-sided demands, we should have a clear intention of what we desire and why. Clarity is the key because we may uncover something about ourselves along the way. The next step is to really feel into the desire. Feel like we already have the end result. Imagine it, dream it, see it, feel it. Don't let any negative thoughts get in the way; otherwise, we will lose our creative momentum. The more we practice, the easier it will become; our desire can and will come to us. It is the natural law of attraction. Remember: This is our creative process, so no blaming anyone or anything if we don't get what we want, when we want it. Just get back on track and focus, focus, focus.

Is this easy? Hell no! Especially when we have a million other thoughts pushing for pole position in our head. It takes practice, like anything new, and may require a whole new way of thinking, as we are so conditioned into believing that we are not worthy and only the lucky ones or the rich ones get what they want.

Creation requires letting go of double-sided demands and taking responsibility for our thoughts. To do that, we have to let in some peace and allow ourselves some space in which creation can grow. It means slowing down and shutting off the internal noise of our own demands. So next time our inner Veruca Salt shows up, demanding results while stamping her impatient feet at us, tell her what millions of kids, adults, and Willy Wonka have wanted to tell her since 1971: "Shut the hell up, Veruca!"

Sacred Acceptance Mantra

I choose this path from a place of love.
I know I am enough, as I am.
I accept there is no need to give any more of myself.
Every aspect of me, as I am, serves me.
I own, accept, and love what is.
This path will lead to a healthier, happier me.
This path with lead to a harmonious, beautiful life,
because I am enough as I am.
I am enough. I am love.

I am blessed with the knowledge that who I am
has nothing to do with success or failure.
I am blessed with the knowledge that the key
to my happiness rests in my heart.
All I need do is surrender.
I am enough. I am love.

I walk this path, knowing a beautiful life is in store for me.
I will accept and embrace whatever comes my way from this moment.
I now realise that hidden inside every challenge is a
wondrous gift of growth and opportunity.
I step forward, knowing the loving bonds
I so desire
begin with me.
I am enough. I am love.

Dream

Night breezes whisper.
Dream a little dream.
Be bold enough to dream.
Be brave enough to dream.
For in your dream state,
secrets are revealed by your soul.
Dream on and don't stop.

I have had crazy success with vision boards over the years. I made my first when I was in the throes of leaving my marriage. I had no idea where I would live, no idea how I could afford it, and no idea about anything, other than survival. What I did have was dreams: dreams of a safe place full of calmness and peace. I dreamed of a home that would be my sanctuary and where I could find myself again. While my head pounded from the panicked thoughts of how I could make it happen, my heart and soul were already off, looking for this sacred space.

I began looking through old magazines, cutting and snipping images of homes and gardens that brought me a great feeling of peace. Slowly, I began to paste them all onto an old canvas. The end result was beautiful. I hung that vision board right in front of my desk at work. I looked at it constantly. I meditated on the images regularly and could see myself moving through the rooms, walking barefoot on the wooden floors and climbing the stairs, moving easily and effortlessly from room to room. In one meditation, I found myself stopped at the bottom of the staircase. I looked at my reflection in a mirror. I was smiling and happy. I looked so relaxed, so fresh, and so alive. That image moved me to tears, as it felt so real. It evoked such passion that it played over and over in my mind, again and again.

Roll on six months, and I was in a home of my own, exactly like the one in my vision board. Everything from the two-storey weatherboard style I loved, to the wooden floors and staircase, the colours on the walls, and the very succulents planted in the garden that exactly matched my vision board. I had not even been out there, physically looking for a home. This home was the first I saw when I was finally ready to make the move. I had found my sanctuary and sacred space ... or did it find me?

My next vision board success was just as crazy as the first. This board was love related and carried images of fairy-tale weddings, a blockbuster love story, sparkling engagement rings, and a knight in shining armour. Again, within six months or so of making this board, the knight appeared; the love was intense and worthy of blockbuster status, and then an engagement ring materialised. There were even grand plans for a fairy-tale wedding in a castle.

Sad to say, this one was fatally flawed, for in my quest to attract blockbuster love, that was unfortunately what I got. Intense as it was, it was sadly not real and didn't last. But there was no denying the vision board exercise had been a success. I have since learned to be very careful what I wish for.

When I next covered my vision board with images of flowers in full bloom, I set the intention for me to bloom as an individual and for my life to bloom in general.

There was no crazy movie stuff on this one, just a heartfelt vision of beautiful, simplistic blooming … and I did; my life did too, in incredible ways. I can honestly say I was transported to one of the most peaceful and creative times in my life, and I bloomed and grew in that period in ways I never thought possible.

Drawing on the memories from that time, I still love to set a vase of fresh pink roses and intoxicating eucalyptus leaves on my desk as I write, to remind me to always bloom.

Sacred Intentions Mantra

Dip into a salt bath, light some candles, and repeat the mantra until you feel the words resonate in your heart and solar plexus:

May the luminous light of the universe shine upon me and
through me until it is dripping from the very tips of my toes.
For I am bold and strong.
I release all fear of moving forward in my life.
I am confident.
I am divine light.
I follow my heart's desires fearlessly.
I am grateful for the lessons I have learned.
I allow ancient memories of my power to surface
so that I may serve my highest good.
I am light. I am love.

Relax in the salt water
long enough to dissolve all negativity.

Shine

When you next look at your reflection,
show some love to the beautiful soul
staring back at you.
You are a spark of divine light.
Be grateful.
Feel blessed.
Then go shine your light in the world.

As I looked at my daughter in her final year of school, my heart filled with love at the stunning young woman before me, full of life and vitality. It was hard to believe twelve years had passed since her first day at school, when I cried as she squinted into the sunshine and the camera pointed at her.

She had been through a lot, though I know not as much as some kids. She moved across the world at the age of six and left friends, family, her school, starting a new life in a new country. At the age of eleven, she experienced the trauma of divorce and all the complications that brings, in terms of logistics, emotions, shame, and anger. But this beautiful daughter of mine, ever graceful, ever caring, ever present, ever selfless, infused her love into every situation and reminded me to constantly smell the roses.

Everything is beautiful when she is around. Life is sweet like fig jam, and we have shared many, many blessings as we have steered through life together. She has so much wisdom and maturity; not one day goes past without me hugging her close and telling her how much I love her. We laugh until our sides feel fit to burst, and we cry, hugging each other like best friends and sisters all rolled into one. She is the cheese to my macaroni, the butter to my toast.

She worried about her final year and grades, but I told her that she cannot be, and never will be, defined by a letter or number. It pains me to see the damage this does to young adults who are robbed of their self-esteem and confidence by hopes of a high school grade, in an already fragile period of life. I reminded her there is never failure in life because we are only ever seeking to find our balance, and no piece of paper will ever have any bearing on how much love I have for her or how much she should have for herself. I told her to never let a piece of paper with a number on it dim her inner light. Yes, it may open some doors, but what use is a smart brain with no love or light to steer it? "Balance, darling, balance", I told her.

I told her she is capable of anything she puts her mind to, but the key to success is happiness. I told her not to let others define happiness for her, not to measure happiness by possessions or job titles, but to measure it by the very emotions she feels as she travels along her path. I reminded her to always follow her heart and that she will be supported in every decision she makes (or doesn't make).

Life is a lesson for us all, and the most humbling part of being a parent is sharing wisdom. Not to dictate, control, or manipulate, but to nurture and allow our children to fine-tune their own music, so they may find harmony in life. For in doing so, they will find themselves. If we are honest and come from a place of love and truth in our roles as parents, we can dissolve the cellular memory of errors in our lineage, those errors we experienced that did not serve us. We can dissolve them with pure love, knowing we have not passed them on to our children but have, instead, learned from them.

All children on this planet are beautiful sparks of creation, and if we can just shine the light from our own hearts and show them the way, then we can all live bright.

Sacred Spark Visualisation

May your light shine on others.

Visualise yourself standing on the summit of the tallest mountain.
Gaze at the wonder of the night sky above and around you.
You are safe and steadfast in your footing,
with the world stretched out below.

Now reach deep into your heart and scoop up pearls of divine love.
Then, like a fisherman casting his nets into the ocean,
scatter the pearls across the night skies.
Cast your loving light into the night skies until
you have illuminated the world.
Cast your loving intentions.
Do not pause to worry.
Your supply is infinite.

Watch as the sky becomes heavy with the weight
of the shimmering pearls of love.
They fill the night sky to bursting point.
Be in awe of the purity of your creation.

Then, as if divinely orchestrated,
see the pearls in the night sky split at their seams.
As they erupt, they shower light on all beings,
drenching them in pure, unconditional love.
Gaze in wonder at the celestial shower of love falling
like luminescent rain across the globe.

On this night, there will be no one left in darkness.
There will be no one untouched by your love.
You are a beacon of magnificent universal light and love.
You are shining your light for all to see and sharing
your love unconditionally for all to feel.
You have planted the seeds of enlightenment in every being.

May you be blessed, beautiful one, for standing
tall, as a fearless example for all to follow.
May you be blessed for sharing your light.

Forgiveness

You are so beautiful.
More so than a calm river on a summer's day.
The most beautiful flower does not come close.
You stand in beauty that is yours and your alone.
Stop judging yourself and others,
and see the miracle you are.

orgiveness was calling me. By that, I mean the word had been popping into my head relentlessly, jumping up and down to be heard. I love the way my higher self stirs me into action; it plants a seed that takes root and won't let go until I face it. Forgiveness is a delicate area of life and one that may touch us gently or harshly. We often hear people resolutely say they will never forgive someone for their actions. Others say they forgive but will never forget. Some just blow us away with their words of forgiveness amidst the most heinous circumstances. One thing is clear: Forgiveness is not something that can be just handed out on a plate. It is one of life's biggest hurdles.

For me, forgiveness was learning to let of go of pain and torment ... and more. I decided firstly that I was not prepared to awaken to this gift of life and then spend another day in which my thoughts, feelings, and actions would be guided by the effects my ex-husband was having on me. It had affected everything in my life; I could feel it in my very core. My cortisone levels were through the roof, and I was running on adrenaline, like a huge pot on permanent boil. Living like that was incredibly unhealthy, on all levels. I knew my heart was under enormous strain, my blood pressure was through the roof, and my emotional stability ... well, imagine a super volcano about to blow and wipe out civilisation.

Never were truer words spoken than those from the Serenity Prayer: "God grant me the serenity to accept the things I cannot change, courage to know the things I can, and wisdom to know the difference". It became my mantra, because no matter what is said by another that causes hurt or anguish, no matter what action they take, no matter how many tears we shed as a result, no matter how far off the rails they push us, there comes a point when the realisation has to set in that we just can't change them. We can't think for them, we can't feel good emotions for them, we can't make them say the good things we want to hear; and we can't control their choices or actions. To attempt to do so just might destroy us in the process.

When I realised that I was never going to be able to change how he treated me, a calmness flooded through me. It was the first step of my awakening to forgiveness. The relief that followed from being able to put down the weight of ongoing drama, anticipation, and dread was enormous. I began to realise that all I had to do was concern myself with *me*. Rather than focus on him, I had to focus on myself. I saw clearly the extent of the things that I could in no way ever change about him, as they were so far out of my control.

I then realised that my feelings of betrayal, hurt, and anger belonged to *me*, which meant that as they belonged to me, they were something that *I* could control. In that moment of enlightenment, my feelings of anger left me almost immediately. I had finally grasped the fact that the feelings of anger were coming from my position of helplessness, and as soon as I realised that *my* feelings were in *my* control, the helplessness was gone. The critical turning point came from the awareness that the emotions were mine, not his, but mine, and that was something I could change … so I did.

There comes a point in the journey of forgiveness where if we strip away all the drama, we find ourselves facing our own emotions. Those we *can* own. Those we *can* change. The biggest leap we can make towards forgiveness is knowing this; when we strip ourselves back to the source, free from all drama and the ego, we will see the chaos surrounding us as something entirely separate from us. If we can see ourselves in this way, then we will see the other person in this way too, and therein lies the key to forgiveness. We are all oneness.

The same energy that made this vast universe also made you, and them, and him, and her, and everyone, and everything. We are all made from the same source energy, and we have the choice to return to the source at any time. Just imagine a newborn baby. It's how we all started off in this world: free from any influence, judgement, or pain. Think of this, and we will see our own beautiful spark of creation and that of all others.

Forgiveness may lead us to experience a new sense of freedom, from which we can live a life in which we shine brightly, once again.

Full Moon Ritual for Letting Go

A full moon offers an incredibly potent opportunity to harness the immense celestial power and cast off all that no longer serves us. It is a time of releasing, cleansing, and purifying.

You will need:
quiet time,
floating candles,
a bowl of water,
matches,
fragrance.

Find a quiet place to perform your full moon ritual. You may like to do this under the direct power of the full moon. How empowering! Create a sacred space by setting out your bowl of water and surrounding it with four candles, placed in the position of north, south, west, and east. You may also like to add flowers and crystals to make a truly beautiful sacred space. As you light each candle, call upon the elemental forces of the earth to activate your ritual:

- north: the element of earth for strength
- east: the element of air to carry away your troubles
- south: the element of fire for purification
- west: the element of water for cleansing

Next, add some fragrance to your sacred space. You may like to have some white sage, cleansing lavender, or eucalyptus oil burning or sprinkled in the water. Adding fragrance heightens the power of the ritual. Sage cleanses negative energy, eucalyptus cleanses feelings of hurt, and lavender cleanses emotional stress. As you light the sage or pour droplets of the essential oil into the water, give thanks to their over soul in acknowledgement of their life force.

Sit quietly and take a few deep breaths. If you cannot see the moon, then in your mind visualise its magnificence.

Visualise the feeling of moonlight falling all around you. Sense yourself being bathed in a cloud of glorious moon dust. You can feel the strong pull of the moon. It is calling you into action.

As you sit quietly, imagine a beam of light extending from the centre of the moon and connecting with your heart centre. A single thread of moonlight now connects you directly to the immense power of the moon. The power of the moon is now being channelled directly to your heart centre.

With this power, you are able to clearly feel and see all that no longer serves you. It is time to release old beliefs, thoughts, and feelings. As you think of each belief, thought, or feeling that you wish to release, place a floating candle upon the water in your bowl and light it. As the flame ignites, affirm, "I let go".

You may wish to affirm, "I let go of self-doubt", "I let go of feeling fearful", "I let go of feeling inadequate". Whatever comes up will be right for you. When all candles have been lit, ask the spirit of earth to ground you and give you strength; also ask the spirit of fire to purify and transmute each negative thought, feeling, or belief to the light with love. Ask the spirit of air to carry each trouble away, and the spirit of water to cleanse you from the effects of all that no longer serves you.

Give thanks for the lessons you have been taught and the gifts of expansion offered, and then affirm:

I let go, I let go, I let go.
I am light. I am love. I am whole. I am complete.

Once you have released all you wish to, visualise the single beam of light from the moon slowly retracting from your heart space. You remain enveloped in the glorious cloud of moon dust. This serves to remind you of the power of the full moon and of the power you now have within you to help you make positive changes.

Bathe in the blissful moonlight (real or imagined) for as long as you feel necessary, and when you are ready, give thanks to Mother Earth, the elements, and the moon for their assistance.

Gratitude

Call to mind a memory
that makes you smile.
Recall the wonderful
feeling of that moment.
As your spirits lift,
feel your heart expand with
love and gratitude.

I spent my childhood in the early 1970s with warm summers, playing in long grass and climbing trees with my best friend, Craig. His mother kept an amazing garden, and I recall the deep purple colour of the foxglove flowers that grew in a certain part of her garden. I can see myself sitting there now, in the long green grass. I often wondered what would happen if I stuck my fingers inside those foxgloves. These flowers were scary and beautiful, all at the same time. Were they really poisonous? Would I die? Or was that simply a story concocted to protect the beautiful flowers from inquisitive children? I loved the white lupins, with petals shaped like little pods, just asking to be popped, and I adored the beautiful, bountiful lilac bushes. The fragrance was intoxicating, as was the sight of the bumblebees that buzzed lazily from flower to flower and the floating butterflies that converged on the lilacs. I could sit for what seemed like hours surrounded by the colours, the fragrances, and the sound of the buzzing bumblebees.

Craig perfected his Chinese burn technique on me but also taught me how to tie my shoelaces. I have vivid memories of sitting by his doorstep while he climbed the tree out front. He watched me try over and over again, tears falling, until at last I did it. We would play hide-and-seek in his garden, and every time, it would feel like a new adventure. We loved pretending to be characters from our favourite television shows. He would be Steve Austin, the Six Million Dollar Man, and I would be Lyndsay Wagner, the Bionic Woman. We would role-play until dinner time and race to get back to play as soon as possible.

I have my happiest childhood memories from that time with Craig and his family, and such is my love of the memory of being in his garden that to this day, it is one of the places I regularly retreat to in my meditation practice. It was and remains for me a place of peace, calmness, beauty, fun, and happiness all at once.

Summers were summers, and winters were winters, in the best possible way back then: from burning holes in paper scraps with a magnifying glass in the summer, to rolling snowballs as big as cars in the winter. Sometimes, we would roll a snowball so far and so big that we couldn't move it any farther . . . which was usually in the middle of the road, much to the dismay of drivers. There was always something to do, but memories of playing in that garden during summer, with our pale (almost blue) skin turning the colour of golden syrup, fill me with nothing but wonderful gratefulness; those happy, happy times are etched into my soul.

I am so grateful for the gift of living those happy times, the gift of my memory, the gifts of my senses for capturing the sights, sounds, smells, and feelings from that time and preserving them so well, ready to be replayed at any time. From recalling one of my favourite memory gifts, I can see clearly that gratitude comes in many shapes and forms. It is always a bearer of abundance and completely grounding in its simplicity. Gratitude teaches us that our lives are already bountiful, if only we pause long enough to see with our hearts.

Gratitude Prayer

In honour of my divine creation,
I recognise the beauty that is me.
For I am a rose petal touched by heaven.
No one has the right to judge me, nor I them,
for a creation by the hand of the divine cannot be
negatively compared to anything or anyone.

In honour of my divine creation,
I see the beauty that surrounds me,
the pulsating, vibrating energetic mass that is life.
May I never stop observing all that passes before me, enriching my life,
coaxing me to savour every moment.

In honour of my divine creation,
I feel the beauty of this experience called life,
this wondrously tactile journey.
May I wholly appreciate the gift of touch from another
and the gift of touch to another.

In honour of my divine creation,
I never cease to accept all that I am and all that is,
for with only one destination, a wasted journey
in the dark is just that: wasted.
May I celebrate my existence and release myself from all falsehoods.
I am living, breathing, gratitude.
I am love. I am.

Recognition

Remember that you are incredible, beautiful,
talented, funny, smart, caring,
loving, capable, powerful, sensual,
and oh, such a blissful and wonderful creation.
Own it!

I'm a firm believer that nothing in life is accidental or simply a coincidence. While I have not always held this belief, in hindsight, it was certainly no coincidence that I found myself looking at a website where people anonymously shared secrets. I had not gone looking for it, so it must have found me. In any event, I was strangely drawn to this online confessional of sorts. I had never expressed my unhappiness in any form, never mind put it into words to tell someone else, but it was to this online "soul friend" that I confessed my secret. My secret was that I desperately wanted to escape the life I led. I was a shell of a person, seeking a hero to scoop me up, love me, and shelter me from the storm that raged in my life, and so I confessed to this online forum my most intimate desires. There was more. You see, I had pinned all of my hero hopes on a certain individual, only he didn't know and wouldn't know because I would never tell him. I thought I was in love. Dumb? Absolutely! But there I was, caught and held fast by the torture of unreciprocated love. Then one day, I received an anonymous reply from my online soul friend that changed everything:

"Unreciprocated love. It is the most incredible thing undeniably, and the most exhausting. To not be with them is sweet torture. But you just have to be faithful in what you know in your heart. Hold on to what he has told you and the connection you have. Souls that touch so strongly are hard to resist, but there could be many other things involved that you don't yet know. Only the universe does, but the universe has its own timetable. It does not listen to impatience. It will happen in its own time. It will happen when you least expect it, but not until you experience the things you have to experience in life. Just know that what is meant for you will be there. On the universe's timetable. Not yours."

If you have ever had a crush on someone, loved someone from a distance, or been in a loveless relationship, then you will know the all-consuming pain of unreciprocated love. Yet receiving this response was an instant game changer for me. The universe had just engaged with my desire to be rescued and had delivered highly evocative words, direct from this soul friend. I saw in that moment I had no connection to my unwitting hero, and he hadn't told me anything because he had no idea what was going on. I saw in that moment there were indeed other things involved, and because of that, he just could not be the hero I longed for. I had tortured myself with longing and impatience, hoping, praying for something outside of myself, and if this was not going to change on my own indeterminable timetable, then I could be doing this forever. And just when I least expected, I was set free from the unhealthy attachment I had formed to my unwitting hero, all by the words of a stranger who had spoken straight to my soul.

Charlotte Bronte wrote in *Evening Solace*, "The human heart has hidden treasures, in secret kept, in silence sealed; the thoughts, the hopes, the dreams, the pleasures, whose charms were broken if revealed." From disclosing my secret, the charms were broken, and I was at once released from their ethereal grip. I could look clearly at where I was and what *I* could do to move forward. That was the point in my life when I took the first real steps, albeit baby steps, to change my life by changing the way I thought.

Of course, I didn't go from baby steps to running a marathon, and just as my soul friend told me all those years ago, there would be many years of life experience to follow. No doubt, there will be many more to come too, but my life had at last been blessed with the hero I sought all those years ago: the hero who scooped me up and guided me safely through the storms, and the hero who continues to fill me with love today. This was the very person who taught me to "just own yourself." That hero is the person who looks back from the mirror. I needed a hero, and I found one in me, all thanks to the words from an anonymous soul friend who shared hidden treasures from their own heart and delivered them to me, right on the universe's timetable.

Sacred Creation Blessing

Too afraid of the light,
too afraid of destruction before experiencing life,
the tight bud remains closed to the world until
a protective exterior splits to reveal but a glimpse of the beauty inside.
Light infiltrates the broken seal,
and the miracle inside is charmed from the safety of its cocoon.

Be released from your protective exterior and
light up the world with your divine beauty.
Embrace the strength from which you are created.

Too long has this bloom been contained.
Too long has the world been denied this beauty.
With divine guidance, thirty-two petals unfold
with courageous and miraculous precision.
For those who are invested, their hearts are touched by
the beautiful splendour, colour, and scent that announce
to the world: This beauty has finally bloomed.

Thirty-two petals unfurl, intoxicating, captivating, gentle, and radiant.
Thirty-two petals contain the blueprint of creation.
Thirty-two petals stand strong against the elements, embracing the light
to send forth happiness into the hearts of all who look upon them.
And when night falls and darkness descends, they
do not close and hide themselves away,
for there is splendour to be witnessed in the heavens above; there is
fulfillment to be had by this joyful bloom under the diamond skies.

Thirty-two petals of universal love: tokens to nourish the soul.
Thirty-two petals: symbols of unique perfection,
authenticity, grace, and surprise.
32 petals: evocative, magical miracles of nature.
Thirty-two petals of life and soul contain the
power to heal, soothe, and comfort.
Thirty-two petals, captivating and tender, are the
embodiment of the feminine blueprint.

May you see within you the strength of a rose,
the thirty-two elements of the divine goddess.
May you embrace the divine feminine within you
to light up the world like
sunlight upon an endless field of roses in summer.
May you be blessed with the certainty that
you are radiant and captivating,
and may you never deny your true beauty.

Abundance

You are so beautiful in every possible way.
You make the birds sing and the days special.
There are not enough words to say how
much light you bring to this world.
You are everything, and in my heart, you will stay.

Autumn is my favourite time of the year, and of course, it is harvest time, a time of bountiful supply of fruits, vegetables, and grains. The leaves begin to turn until there is an abundance of amber, gold, flame red, and burnt orange leaves to be enjoyed. Cool enough to sleep and still warm enough to enjoy the outdoors, it is the beginning of a slow slide into winter. Everything seems to quieten down a touch too, as if Mother Earth has taken a deep breath, and a relaxed calm has fallen with the leaves.

As I watch trees blowing in the wind, I see autumn-coloured leaves break free and float to the ground. Freedom, I think, freedom for the leaves breaking free from the tree, and freedom for the tree casting off the leaves that are dying and no longer serve it. It reminds me how wonderful it has felt at times in my life to shake things off and be free of them, of things that served their purpose and were no longer required. In their fall, they nourished me with wisdom, just like the leaves falling to the ground nourish the earth and are essential for the growth of the tree.

I watch as the wind picks up and the trees bend some more. Branches shake, and leaves are scattered. As I focus on one particular tree, mature, it stands firm while its branches bend in the wind. I think of how easy it is in life to bend and flex with challenges and changing conditions when we are grounded and steadfast in our own identity, yet how easy it is to become uprooted and tossed to the elements if we only have a shallow grasp of our own identity. Surface dwellers are uprooted too often in life and in nature. We can learn a lot from the earth and from observing nature. It is at times our greatest teacher; after all, mankind has been on earth for such a short time.

There are treasures to be found in the simplest of forms when we spend a moment observing nature and experiencing silence. For some, it is a struggle to simply observe in silence. For many, silence is uncomfortable and weird. Yet this is the time when answers come with ease. Clarity and epiphany moments burst forth, and we feel peace in our hearts before returning to the noise of the world. It is easy in moments of silence and when in nature to see the abundance we are surrounded by.

The golden autumn leaves are a reminder to look for and recognise the cornucopia of abundance that is all around us. When we think of lack, we act like a magnet attracting that very energy. When we think of abundance, we attract more of the same. While we may not all see trees as our teacher, or the autumn leaves as rubies falling at our feet, consider instead the abundance that is in the gift alone of having sight to see such beauty, the gift of how our brain translates the beautiful images into jewels before our eyes.

We should never stop appreciating the simple reminders of abundance that are all around us. "Every moment of your life is infinitely creative and the universe is endlessly bountiful. Just put forth a clear enough request, and everything your heart desires must come to you." writes Shakti Gawain in *Creative Visualisation: Use the power of your imagination to create what you want in your life.*

Gaia Invocation

Deep in the earth, life waits.
Water, air, and nutrients combine to nourish and
coax movement from the darkness.
Slowly, a magical creation pushes through what
seems to be an impenetrable structure.
Ahhhh, the sunlight gently kisses the tip of this newborn.
Intuitively, the energy is captured by an invisible force,
and life bursts forth to colour our world.

Provider of food and medicine,
provider of clean fresh air,
nurturing, bountiful Mother Earth, we thank you.

High in the mountains, a mother's arms are stretched wide.
She captures rain as it falls, snow as it melts.
She scoops and directs this across the planet,
giving life, cleansing the way.
Ahhhh, the thirsty earth and the thirsty animals drink up her gift.
Intuitively, the water is captured by an invisible
force, and life bursts forth in its wake.

Provider of life,
provider of cleansing, nourishing water,
nurturing, bountiful Mother Earth, we thank you.

Deep in the ocean, the darkness soothes.
Like a child within a mother's womb,
life is contained, protected, and all elements are in balance.
Ahhhh, the darkness soothes the creatures and
carries them silently in its hold.
Intuitively, they respond to silent wisdom, and life bursts from the depths.

Provider of darkness,
provider of power and creation,
nurturing, bountiful Mother Earth, we thank you.

Gaia, Mother Earth, we give thanks for this beautiful planet
and the trust you have placed in our hearts.
May we honour and respect this precious creation.
May we have courage to protect the lifeline
which supports our very existence.
May our gratitude and love heal that which we have broken.

Empowerment

Like a blind newborn bird,
you call into the world.
What is it you seek?
Do not remain helpless, like a flightless bird.
For that which brings you sustenance
may also consume you.
Spread your wings and fly.
Recognise your power.

The pain in my pelvis and hips is torturous. My entire sacral area is aching. I can feel my insides twisting and turning, my hips and legs bending and stretching in ways that make me want to curl up into a ball and scream, "No more! No more! No more!" Through the tears that are falling and the sobs that are coming thick and fast, I decide right there and then: *No more.*

I see myself as a magnificent, luminous being floating in the timeless abyss of space. White light beams from my entire being, and I stand tall in my own strength. Around me, I see cords and chains. They are attached to my body and floating far off into the darkness. They vary in thickness, colour, and texture, from thin gold threads to strong steel chains. I understand that they represent male energy, male energy from those I have traded my body and soul to in this incarnation. As I see this unfolding in front of me, I am strong and resolute. There is to be no more of this. My hands move across the cords and chains as I sever each one. Some chains are so strong and thick that in my mind's eye, I see an acetylene torch cut through the metal, until I am free at last. I feel immediate release and freedom and cry what feels like a million tears: tears for being so naive, tears of humiliation, and now tears of joy for the awakening I have just experienced.

I decide in that instant that my body will never again be a haven for loveless sex, nor my soul a haven for loveless relationships. I call back my energies, pieces of me that I traded in a fruitless search for love, in a fruitless search of belonging. I know that I will never accommodate loveless sex or loveless relationships again. I am a beautiful being of light, deserving of love.

My energy healing session is complete, and I have just experienced an incredible awakening and shift. I now know freedom like never before.

I wrote these words immediately following a truly incredible session with my energy healer. I instantly felt like a bird being set free from a cage. During the session, I had the incredible realisation of just how much I had given of my body and soul throughout my life, by force, by being manipulated, or to survive. But no matter what the reason, I saw that I had permitted this to go on. I saw that I had subconsciously accepted this as my fate, and that was the line-in-the-sand moment. I had come too far to continue like this. No more.

The reality is, we all give of ourselves to procure something; it is something we all do. It can be happening across all relationships in our lives, including business relationships, friendships, family members, and partners. We need to look closely at our relationships and examine whether we are trading any aspect of our self, and if so, we need to begin to ask, "What am I trading, and why am I trading?" Living in this shadow side of the archetypal prostitute fosters unhealthy beliefs and actions. Piece by piece, we can be torn apart on a soul level. We can be left asking ourselves why we feel devalued when we are living as we only know how. Our soul always knows why, even if we don't. We need to listen to those feelings, to our subconscious calling.

It is important to examine our lives for this trend so we can stop it and instead begin to set healthy boundaries that will serve and protect us on all levels. Power also comes from having the ability to say no in a way that clearly defines our boundaries and calls for respect. Unfortunately, for many of us, no is something we cannot easily say. No one teaches us to set boundaries in life. We may be fortunate to learn by observing healthy boundaries in action, but if not, we are left to stumble through and are ultimately left to face the consequences. Unfortunately, for some, despite saying no, the other party does not want to hear it, and so we may find ourselves manipulated into retracting our power by virtue of our actions, while our soul screams from within to be heard.

Awareness is the key to breaking free from any cage that we find our self held within. Simply become aware, and the awareness will stay with us, calling us into action. For only then can we experience the miracle of freedom on all levels and live a life filled with love of self.

Sacred Blessing from Goddess Ishtar

Women of the world, I grant you strength and courage
to cease the giving and trading of your light.
All divine children, now awaken to your divine
feminine and masculine power.
With grace, set healthy boundaries to protect your body, mind, and soul.
I release rivers of love through your veins, and you are now
blessed with the power to say no to the demands of others.
I will assist you in severing all cords of
attachments that no longer serve you.
I bless you with profound inner strength.
I grant you clarity so you may see your glorious worth
and value as divine light beings upon this earth.
I honour your divine essence and immerse you in a pool of
universal love, where my light permeates every cell of your body.
Be guided by love.
Be strong while standing in a place of light.
So be it.

Balance

Hush, my child,
Be still.
You demand so much of yourself,
yet forget yourself all at once.
Softly, softly is the key.
Be still.
All is well.

At the age of forty-five, I made a life-changing decision. The habit of more than three decades was stamped out in the blink of an eye. Something in me just shifted in a momentous way. Something that required no cognitive weight at all just burst from within and changed my life in an instant. I stopped drinking.

At the age of forty-five, something inside me just said, "Enough." It was akin to receiving a divine delivery, a symbolic message in a bottle. There was no premeditation; there was no plan. Not a single thought had been directed towards giving up the toxic elixir, and yet there I was, standing at the precipice of a new life without my oldest "friend."

My relationship with alcohol began around thirteen years old, after my father suddenly died. Looking back, it was a means to block out trauma, a means to be swallowed up in a black abyss, where I didn't have to think, feel, or do. My relationship with alcohol continued throughout a very long and turbulent period of my life. I sought solace in many a bottle of wine to seek refuge from abuse. I returned again and again to the strange safety that the black abyss could offer me. It was, of course, a coping mechanism, and while I didn't drink habitually, I did use it to escape mentally, physically, and emotionally from the chaos. It was simply a far easier road to take at the time, a friendlier demon to face. It was a very welcome distraction.

After spending years in an abusive relationship, I realised that I would very likely die if I couldn't find the strength to take steps to escape from that life. I needed clarity to create change, and so I replaced alcohol with courage. I meditated, journaled, and took regular energy clearing sessions. With calmness came the clarity and courage I desperately needed. After taking control of my life, it changed considerably for the better, and I no longer sought shelter in the arms of a bottle of wine. But instead of wiping it out completely, I continued drinking alcohol as a reward. It was a reward for a hard week, a reward for the hard times, and it was socially acceptable and a norm in every setting. It was everywhere and a part of everyone I knew.

Then one day, I noticed an old pattern had reared its head. I was again relying on the distraction that alcohol offered rather than the courage that was required to deal with something at that time. As soon as I recognised that, the symbolic bottle washed up against me, nudged my feet, and the message I unfurled from inside said, "Enough."

In that moment, I saw how much of a distraction from life alcohol had offered. I realised just how many things I had covered with a blanket and put in the too-hard, too-painful-to-deal-with basket. I was dancing with the devil of distraction (distraction being nothing more than avoidance in disguise).

I saw the damage to my health. I saw the damage to my finances. I saw that I had given my power to it. I saw through it all, and in that moment, I was so grateful to be alive, so grateful to have finally received complete clarity, and just like that, I was done.

I felt I had just signed and sealed a sacred contract to honour me, myself. There would be no going back. It was my turn to take to the dance floor again, this time with the Divine instead of the devil of distraction.

Half-Moon Rising Mantra

The half-moon reminds us that we are all equal parts light and shade, yin and yang, and masculine and feminine. One cannot exist without the other, and like the cycles of the moon, we are entwined with the cycles of life. We traverse periods of light and shade, balance and imbalance, but we are always the embodiment of oneness.

I am the stillness of winter and the vibrancy of summer.
I am the cold of ice and the heat of the searing sun.
I am the rising flood waters and the parched, arid desert.
I am the loyal lover and the eternal free spirit.
I am fluid as a river and solid as granite.
I am the light of day and the dark of night.
I am the embodiment of the divine masculine and feminine.
I am the yin and yang.
I am the rising sun and the setting sun.
I am the new moon and the full moon.
I honour the rhythms and cycles of life,
the dance of the light and shade.
I honour the ebb and flow in my search for balance.
I am all stages of life
and all elements of the cosmos at once.
I am the half-moon rising.
I am perfect balance.
I am oneness with the universe.

Love

Let the sunshine flow from your heart
out into the world,
touching the hearts and souls of many,
leaving a glow,
a memory,
a spark.
When tomorrow comes, do it all again,
and never cease to stop.
Let the sunshine flow,
unabated,
unfaltering,
unstoppable.

"To love another is something like prayer and can't be planned, you just fall into its arms because your belief undoes your disbelief." wrote Anne Sexton in the poem *Admonitions to a Special Person.*

Do you believe in love, or has disbelief gripped your heart in its vice-like grip? There is nothing like the feeling of being head-over-heels in love. Do you remember the feeling? Maybe you are experiencing it right now. The butterflies in your stomach? The flushed face and breathlessness catching you unawares? Falling asleep with a smile on your face, your heart bursting with love, then waking up to the day ahead, excited beyond words by the promise of endless possibilities? "Today when I awoke I walked into the garden to be met by the most beautiful perfume. It reminded me of you, how beautiful you are. You are graceful, vibrant, colourful and that's how I started my day … with thoughts of you." T. Farrah said to the woman he loved, me.

Love is the most incredible feeling in the world. Love is natural, wholesome bliss. Everything and anything is possible when love takes us in its arms. We abandon all fears, cast caution to the wind, and float off into an endless sea of euphoria. Held in love's embrace, comparable only to heaven on earth, we bare our hearts and souls. Yet if we are not in a relationship with a special someone, we generally deny ourselves all of that excitement, elation, and the childlike jumping from our slumber to savour all that the new day brings. Instead, we press pause and wait. We wait with baited breath for the day to come when we will experience that rare bliss with someone special … someone … someday.

But we should not deny ourselves such joy, nor anyone else for that matter, because we are always in a relationship. We are always in a sacred relationship of self and spirit, and spirit never drops the ball, never misses the mark, never ever falls out of love with us.

We will always manage to find a million other things more beautiful than ourselves, but not in the eyes of spirit. When the day dawns, we see a sleepy-eyed groaning mess crawl to the bathroom with one eye opened in a futile attempt to block out the light of day. Spirit sees only an angel awaken with beauty like a glistening blue lake. When we are feeling sad or upset, spirit wants nothing more than to hold us for as long as possible. When we feel clumsy, frazzled, and out of sorts, spirit sees only elegance, sparkle, and poise. Spirit starts every day with thoughts of us and bids us to awaken more beautiful than any rainbow. Spirit never doubts how special we are and never stops telling us this is one relationship that will last forever.

Love is devotion in its purest form, and the best kind is that which will awaken our soul, tend to our sorrow with compassion, and bring peace to our hearts and minds. However, when love ends, a world of pain generally follows. Gradually, the initial hurt and anger may turn to sadness, then dullness, then healing. It's all healing, as this is spirit tending to our wounds. When we have reclaimed the gifts of peace and love of self, we are ready to love again, but we must not forget the one who always loves us through thick and thin, through relationship after relationship, who whispers words of encouragement to our soul as we sleep each night, who looks into and through our beautiful eyes and only sees heaven. That is spirit.

Love should not be saved or packed away in a box like good china and only brought out for special occasions. Beautiful, soulful love should be shared and shown in every possible way, in every relationship, enough to make the birds sing and the days special. At the end of the day, spirit will be always be waiting to hold us all through the night, ready for a new day full of endless possibilities. If we awaken to this knowledge, then we can experience this deep level of soul love every day of our lives. If we can let ourselves be nourished and nurtured in this sacred relationship with spirit, then any relationship thereafter will be blessed with lavish abundance.

Old Souls Visualisation

This visualisation will invoke the elementals, who will call to your soulmate using the wind, trees, flowers, rivers, and lakes. Journey now with the elemental realm and experience love through their eyes. Your heart will be blessed, and your radiance will shine bright for all to see, as the visualisation joins the masculine and the feminine energies. Place both hands on your heart as you read:

I visualise the grass under my bare feet. It is soft and refreshing.
I look up into the trees and feel shards of sunlight on my skin.
I am walking in the forest and feeling intense peace.
It is a beautiful place to be, and today I feel beautiful.
My hair hangs free, and I wear a truly gorgeous ivory dress
which skims over my bare feet.
I am to be married here today in the forest, and
I feel the happiness soar in my heart.

I walk towards a clearing bathed in golden
sunlight, and there he waits, my king.
My heart bursts with joy just seeing him there.
He is waiting for me with his hands outstretched, my beautiful soulmate.
I visualise my heart. It spills brilliant green light from within,
radiating like the brightest emerald I have ever seen.
At my heart's core is brilliant white light,
divine light that bursts forth when my hands take his.
From deep green edges to brilliant white at its core,
my emerald heart shines and sparkles.

He looks resplendent, waiting there for me.
Strong and proud. My protector.

We marry there in the forest, and it appears all of heaven
and the angels have come to grant us their blessing.
This is truly a day of highest love and joy.
I have never felt so complete, so in love, and so at peace.
The forest is bathed in light, and it shines
upon our heads and fills our bodies.
We are one in the eyes of heaven and earth.
He is my true love, my destiny, my soulmate, my everything.
So be it.

Clearing

Beautiful one,
Is your vision clouded by dirt and dust?
Are your ears clogged with mud?
Do you bend under the weight of
things seen and unseen?
The choice is yours to put down the burdens you carry,
to wash away the mud, dirt, and dust.
Cleanse your body, mind, and soul of the disguise you wear
and be radiant once more.

Cleanliness is next to godliness, so they say. We all have big cleanups and clear-outs, but what does it mean when the universal energies take hold of us and the all-purpose cleaner? I recall many a time being taken under the universal wing and placed into a state of constant motion of cleaning body, mind, spirit, and home. Intuitively, I could feel where the blockages were, as if some ethereal force was pulling me here and there, while in my ear, they whispered, "Here, here, clean this, let go of that, deal with this."

Whenever this occurs, it's like trying to clear up before a big event or when a guest is coming to stay. Only this cleaning house is always deep and touches the very core of my being. It feels like I'm being prepared for something big, as if big change is coming, a new approach to life, an awakening … a new and evolved me. It's always exciting.

Nothing is left untouched when I am in these states of catharsis. I eat nothing but clean, unprocessed foods, drink water by the litre, meditate more deeply and frequently. I clear out cupboards, drawers, shelves, desks, electronic files, and contacts; I even shampoo the carpets. I brush, scrub, and purge spaces with sound and incense and purify almost everything that moves. I deal with all manner of things that need doing and say things that need to be said. I release people who need to be released, for their own growth and for mine. I allow what I feel is right to be done. None of it is planned at all; it all just takes place, and I feel that I am truly going with the flow of energies that are whirling and swirling around me in a dance. "Keep up." they say. "Keep up. See what you have become attached to and let attach to you. More to clear, more to clean."

Purification of body, mind, and spirit can only lead to one thing, higher vibration, and that is a good thing because it brings each of us closer to the source, which is exactly where the collective consciousness is heading. You may see evidence of the shift happening all around you. Maybe you are feeling it also. People are no longer willing to tolerate the dramas or the circumstances that weigh heavy on the soul. They are depositing the drama in search of their dharma. All of the slimy surface material that so many people define themselves by, is being scraped away, as the vibration of the higher energies, closer to the source, intensifies. For people who are not ready to have their inner self shown to others, that process may be abrasive and painful.

We are moving more rapidly into a world where goodwill, humility, and love for others will quickly overtake self-obsession and materialistic clutter. As we do so, all of this universal direction to clean house is a clear message to get things in order. Take care of what needs to be done. Take ownership. Dispose of excess. Dispose of drama. Sort our finances. Complete things. Clear our body, mind, and spirit of all that weighs us down and dims our light. Open our eyes to the real drama that is going on all around us, and help others. We all have a part to play in the change that is needed. And the energies keep swirling . . .

Fire and Water Clearing Mantra

The Celtic goddess Brigid offers you a powerful fire and water mantra to help you reach your highest potential. She offers this mantra so that you may be cleansed of all impurities and stand tall in truth and integrity:

Cleansing, clearing fire. Passionate and purging.
Warm me, cleanse me, shelter me.
In your glow, I am safe and protected.
In your consumption, I am reminded of my fragility.
In your destruction, I am part of the cycle of
life, returned to where I began.
In your arms, a spectacular dance entrances me
until you remind me of your strength and force me from your grip.
Such is the fire of life.

Water flowing, water falling, water raging, water still.
Cleansing, clearing water. Pure and refreshing.
Wash over me. Wash through me.
Cleanse me from within.
In your stillness, I bathe, relaxed and soothed.
In your fall and flow, I am refreshed and rejuvenated.
In your rage, I am tossed and tumbled, lost in your power
until in your arms, I am carried effortlessly
and placed softly at the shore.
Such is the flow of life.

May I awaken to discovery.
May I accept my fragility and power on this journey of dreams.
May forgiveness and gratitude enrich my life.
May I love with all-consuming passion, always.

Grace

Take my heart
and show me how to serve.
Take my mind
and show me how to serve.
Take my senses
and show me how to serve.
Take my hands
and show me how to serve.

What do you say to a beautiful soul who teaches you the meaning of unconditional love? What do you say to a beautiful soul who teaches you that beauty shines from your very soul? What do you say to a beautiful soul who teaches you the true meaning of respect and offers your heart comfort on a level never experienced before? "Thank you" does not seem adequate, and perhaps that's because there are just no words in existence that adequately describe the incredible joy such people bring to our lives. While beautiful people may come and go in our lives, their indelible imprint is left on our hearts forever. Like soulful musical notes, their energy resonates within our own energy, transfers through us to others, and plays continual, sweet melodies in our psyche, lovingly soothing and comforting us for all eternity. For beautiful people such as this, no words of appreciation are required. They simply do all they do from a place of pure love, asking nothing in return, for they are secure in their own heart, head, thoughts, and beliefs. There is no dependency, no expectations. There is no attachment to outcome, just pure love from the security of self, and where there is no ego, there is only love.

Expressing appreciation is a societal norm; however, an *expectation* of appreciation is nothing more than the ego at play, and that can cause mayhem in relationships. We are taught as children to be grateful whenever something is done for us, but with that comes the creation of "expectation", which is nothing more than a hole that some need filled. From that hole grew the concept of "ungrateful" and then followed "punishment". There are all manner of choices and decisions we may make that will affect or influence another, without the other party even knowing what has been done, without the other party even asking for anything, never mind the fact that the receiving party may have no idea of what level of appreciation is expected to be given.

Take, for instance, someone who chooses to go to work every day to earn a living. They choose to use some of their own money to buy something for the home, their own home. Instead of feeling grateful for the job they have, the ability to earn money and pay bills, and have some money left over to spend, and the pleasure of making their environment more comforting for themselves and others, they become enraged that nobody has said, "Thank you", no one has said, "Thank you for working so hard every day and buying this lovely thing for this home; you're awesome; you're amazing. What would we do without you?" It's crazy, but it happens all the time and on all scales of craziness. An unfulfilled expectation of appreciation can lead to a bad diagnosis of ungratefulness, for which some see the appropriate action is then punishment.

In reality, this is nothing more than an example of the ego begging to be stroked; it is calling out for approval: "Tell me I did good." "Tell me I am wonderful." On and on, the ego will go, always looking for ways to soothe a lack of self-worth, a lack of self-respect, and hurt. An expectation of appreciation is an entirely one-sided game. Before doing anything for anyone, we must be clear about what our actions are really all about. We are always in control of our own choices. We always have a choice to say no. We always have the ability to negotiate for something in return beforehand if need be. So before proceeding with whatever action, we must be sure we know why we are really doing something and that we are happy to do it unconditionally. We must be sure that our ego isn't standing in the wings, waiting with its soapbox poised, ready to deliver a sermon to the unappreciative masses.

There is no point in doing something for another if all we want in return is our ego stroked. There is no point in buying something for someone if all we want is something in return; again, that is stroking the ego. There is no point in do, do, doing, if at the end of the day (or ten years from now), we are going to ask, "What about me? Nobody ever appreciated me." We all have a choice: to do or not to do. We should ask ourselves, am I doing this unconditionally?

Charles Stanley wrote in his *Handbook for Christian Living*, "When service is not others-orientated, it becomes self-orientated, and the result is obvious. Suddenly everything becomes mine, and territorialism creeps in. When that happens, you can be sure that service is motivated not by a desire to love people through serving them but by a desire to meet one's own needs for attention, fulfillment, or release from the guilt of the past."

When we approach life, giving and doing for ourselves and others from a place of love, the ego stands no chance. This is what personal responsibility means. It is accepting that whatever choice we make, whatever action we take, it is ours and ours alone, no matter who it affects or benefits. Our choices are born from self. When actions come from a place of self-worth and self-respect, no appreciation is needed because the ego has been squashed. With ego out of the picture, there is no expectation for anything, no dependency ever. It simply cannot exist at the same time as love. Just imagine a world where people help others with no expectations, no agendas, and where no ego stands in the wings with a soapbox poised.

Be generous. Be as generous and giving as possible, every day, and expect nothing in return. We will see a radical change for the better in ourselves and everyone around us. It is contagious. Imagine a world of personal responsibility and of ownership. Imagine unconditional love as the societal norm. Imagine a world of beautiful souls. Imagine …

Full Moon Mantra

Close your eyes and visualise a beautiful, luminous full moon. Focus on the white cleansing power radiating from the moon. Sit quietly and pay attention to your breathing until you feel very relaxed. When you are ready, repeat the mantra three times. Visualise cleansing light removing all that does not serve your highest good. Imagine your cares and worries floating effortlessly into space, like paper lanterns illuminating the night sky. Watch as they join the stars and are transmuted into heavenly energy, while on earth your love flows freely in service.

I am a being of love and light.
Under the power of the moon, my cares and worries
are set free into the night sky.
I ask that they be transmuted with love into heavenly energy.

Free from their weight, I feel liberated and radiant.
I sparkle from within and feel a deep connection to the universe.
I am nourished with goodness.
I send cosmic showers of love to all mankind and Mother Earth.
I am a being of love and light.

With love and light my focus falls to service,
So close your eyes, dearest one.
Let me comfort you.
Let me soothe away your pain.
Be still and content,
for you are in kind hands.

Can you feel my love flow to you?
Can you feel my love move through you?
From the tips of your toes,
my love travels through you,
traversing, ascending, encapsulating,
until your body is flooded with my love.
Let me cleanse away your pain.
Let me heal you with my love.

Close your eyes, dearest one.
Imagine before you a crystal clear waterfall.
The water sparkles as it falls.
Let us walk this path together beside the water
until we feel the cool spray upon our faces
and we reach the edge of the waterfall.

Close your eyes, dearest one.
Trust in me to hold you tight
and keep you safe as
we cross under the waterfall
and find ourselves
behind the crystal clear flow.
Pain knows no place here.

Cleansed by the power of the falls,
refreshed by the cool water,
you are free of pain and distress.
Feel the lightness of your body.
Feel gently swaddled in my love.
Close your eyes, dearest one.
We are home.

Cherish

Be blessed with the vision to see that which needs to be seen,
so that your journey may always be guided in love.
Do not close your eyes, or your heart,
for beauty and magic is all around us.

Kali, the Hindu goddess of endings and beginnings, reminds us of the dance of life. She reminds us not to fear change or loss, but to simply accept the ever-changing whirl of universal energy we are part of.

I have watched friends struggle as their worlds were thrown into chaos by the sudden news of their loved ones facing life-threatening illness (or their actual death). I have seen mediums bringing comfort to so many people who were distressed from the loss of their loved ones and with so many unanswered questions dominating their lives.

I have developed a strong belief about death, one that is so far removed from the beliefs I grew up with. Contrary to hell and damnation threats, I now strongly believe there is nothing to fear about death. As a child, I was terrified by a priest who convinced me that if I told one lie, my heart would turn black, and I would go straight to hell upon death. It is sermons such as this that make people scared of death and of life.

If we only view death in our own two-dimensional way of thinking, we see the process as nothing more than a body dying and the loss of a loved one. Without our mind, however, our bodies don't exist. Without our mind, none of this exists. This book does not exist, these words do not exist without our minds. So why do we believe that death is the end? Think about that. That is an incredible reality. Without our mind, none of this exists. What does that tell you about the power of the mind and the stories we have been fed? Where does the mind even come from, because no scientist, no doctor has ever found the mind? The electrical activity and chemical reactions taking place in the brain are not the mind. Does that open you up to the possibility that we are more than just our bodies, more than just a mind? I hope it does.

The belief that we are more than just a body is what helps people bridge the divide between this earth and their loved ones in spirit. People can say goodbye, for now, with love and hope because to believe that death is not the end is a precious gift. I believe there is more; after all, how big must our ego be if we think that the entire purpose of our miraculous creation is to work, to retire, to die?

My first experience of someone passing on beyond this physical life did not instantly "leave a beautiful sense of their presence like music lingering on." as *The Song of Memory* goes. The sound of my mother's guttural screaming, with the realisation that her husband, my father, was dead in bed beside her, has haunted me since he died. I have never heard any noise come close to that again and hope I never will, but I can honestly say that pain did not come from my father's actual death. For on the night before he died, I recall hugging my father in way that said all that needed to be said, without any words. I have the distinct recollection of knowing that I would not see him again. In that moment of physical connection, I said "goodbye" and "I love you" on a deep soul level. I know he felt it too, I saw it clearly in his eyes.

Instead, intense pain came from the nuclear bomb of other people's emotions that I was then caught up in. A lack of faith and acceptance of there being something more than death and endings, brought immeasurable and seemingly finite trauma to my family.

I believe that when someone dies, they have moved onto somewhere better, that we will see them again, and that they are always by our sides, energetically. To have such a belief is a comfort beyond words. I wish my family had owned such a belief and had shared it with me when my father died. Having such a belief and sharing such a belief can change attitudes and change lives because it provides hope when all else appears lost. We are, after all, here for but a short time, enjoying our physical experience. We just have to be bigger than our egos to believe our incredible journey never truly ends.

Journey between Worlds

The goddess Rhiannon, walker between worlds, invites you on a journey. Visualise this beautiful goddess upon a white horse, standing before you. Feel the power from the horse, this guardian of travel. Be assured that you are safe and protected. The goddess Rhiannon offers you her hand. Meander together, if you so desire, to a place unknown. Once there, you will find the true meaning of love, wisdom, and infinity.

Walk with me, sweet angel.
Take my hand and walk awhile.
Let me show you something beautiful.

Come with me, sweet child,
through the meadow grass,
under skies so blue
to the shade of yonder tree.

Watch with me, sweet soul,
as the sun shines bright like fire into our eyes,
blinding us for the briefest of moments.

Gaze with me, sweet darling,
upon the vision that now stands before you
of a loved one gone before,
here to deliver a message of immense love.

I will wait for you, sweet one,
while you gaze upon their smiling face
and feel immeasurable love pass
between you.

I will stay with you, sweet child,
until you are ready to leave this beautiful moment
between two worlds,
but not until you are ready, not a moment before.

I will walk with you, sweet angel,
through the meadow grass,
under skies so blue,
far from the shade of yonder tree,
with your heart full of joy,
free from pain
and with the lasting memory of something beautiful.

Surrender

When the time comes,
you will know what to do.
Fear hides itself in many forms
and yet can be seen so clearly.
Struggle
morphs
into
surrender,
and bliss rushes in.

Another birthday has come around. Would I ever have predicted I would be where am I now, doing what I am doing and living where I am living? No. No because I've never really been one to map out a plan or set life goals. My birthday also coincides with work performance appraisals. One question always asked is, "Where do you see yourself in the next twelve months?" As always, I answer, "Unsure." because that is the truth. I have absolutely no idea, and I really struggle with long-term future planning.

I remember watching my boss practically explode in front of my eyes when I told him just that.

"How do you overcome challenges if you don't plan and struggle?" he bellowed. "Life is like a game of chess."

I thought it best not to tell him that I was the only member of my school chess club who couldn't play chess. Instead, I told him ever so calmly that I believed some struggles were not meant to be overcome; they were, instead, put in front of us to steer us onto a new path. There is always a choice, I told him: a choice to walk away and try something new rather than killing ourselves by banging our heads against a brick wall a million different ways.

"Life isn't all about challenge." I added, much to his exasperation.

I feel very comfortable with my lack-of-future-planning approach to life. It means I can get to sleep easily every night. I don't chew my fingernails, I don't need Valium, and I don't have to run 10Ks to get a shot of endorphins. Thankfully, I can simply be at peace. Don't get me wrong; it's not that I am reckless or blasé. It's more like a curtain has been drawn on the future for me. I know it is there. I know there is a future, but it's just not something that I worry about. I can't be enticed or ensnared by a promise of what may come. I am a present-moment woman and believe things will come to me; paths will open up at the right time, and I will take action when the time is right.

Of course, everything we do (or don't do) in the present will affect the future. However, there really is no beginning and no end, just a constant state of change. Change doesn't worry me, either, because I have faith that everything will be okay. I trust. I may have no idea what life holds for me, but I do know I have made it this far through myriad life changes and challenges, without any planning. Who knows what the future holds for any of us, really? Yet some people are consumed by planning and challenging themselves and others, while sacrificing all that the present moment has to offer.

For some, life is all about the challenge of shaping or controlling the future and others with it. Sadly, life has a way of cutting short plans. There is a birthday card always missing from my desk, one from my beautiful father. Through his absence, he bestows a very special birthday gift. It is an annual reminder to leave the past behind and not to worry about what is yet to come. I hear him whisper to me, "Remember to hold the gift of the present moment in your hands and in your heart. Live in peace, have faith, surrender, and trust that everything will be okay." And I do.

A Sacred Blessing on This Sacred Journey

Every moment of every day provides the opportunity to change direction. The value of this incredible gift may never be known until the moment when we are breathing our last breath. Be brave. Be bold. Do not waste one more second.

Upon the golden sea
the water carries me
into a golden sunset
upon a sailing ship.

Upon the golden sea
the wind calls to me
beckoning me to the open waters.
"Sail away with me", she whispers.
"Sail away".

Venture to places unknown on this golden sea.
The past is left in the wake behind,
the future is far ahead,
and only your decisions in this present moment
may guide your ship.

With the gift of wind to fill your sails
whenever you are ready to travel,
it is you who shall determine where to next,
upon these golden waters.

May you be blessed at every step
of your journey throughout this lifetime.
May you see golden sunsets,
experience freedom,
and travel where your heart beckons.
May your eyes reflect the beauty you find
in every man, woman, and child,
And may your days and nights be illuminated with love.

Bliss

Ahhhhhh,
Aanandha.
Sacred, blessed bliss:
the state from which
creation is born
and to which we will return.
Meanwhile, we search for it everywhere
in between,
blissfully unware it resides
within.
Always has.
Always will.
Ahhhhhh,
Aanandha.

anging in my wardrobe is a dress that I have never worn. That's not an uncommon thing for women, I know, but this one is a wedding dress. When I bought it, it represented everything blissful in my life ... or so I thought. I came to understand that everything I held to be blissful was really only elements of life that I considered would bring me bliss if they all came together, especially wedded bliss. We've all done it: "I will be happy when this happens." "I will be blissfully happy when x, y, z happens." Don't get me wrong; it is never wrong to dream, and we must never stop, but I was so caught up in my projection of the blissful life I yearned for that I was living and breathing it. As powerful as that creative process was, the truth was that my dream life was way out of step with my actual reality. It had gotten out of hand. My dream life and my reality were poles apart. I was living fully in the dream, ungrounded and completely unaware of where I was headed, like Dorothy in *The Wizard of Oz*. Thankfully, like Dorothy, I made it home, but I never got to wear the wedding dress.

As you can imagine, the engagement ended, but I still had a balance to pay on the wedding dress. No one ever thinks they are going to return a wedding dress when they sign the contract to have it made, and so I found myself driving to the dress shop to pay off the balance and collect the dress, for a wedding that was not to be. I held myself together in the store while the sales assistant rang through the final payment and fetched my dress, and the staff wished me good luck for the big day. I made it to the car, threw the dress in the back seat, and burst into tears. My dreams of my hero, of blissful love, a life partner, safety, and security, lay in the back seat of my car with the remnants of my bliss, my Aanandha. It was devastating, but I was thankfully back in the real world and totally grounded. I have often described the moment in which I realised my dream was not my reality, as being hit by a huge wrecking ball, squarely in the solar plexus. Thank you, universe, for hitting me and hitting me real hard. It was to be a major turning point in life for me.

I am forever grateful for the many lessons learned from all that transpired from the relationship itself, including the ending (as hard as it was), and with my relationships with my family and friends. It was a time that was instrumental for me in finding my voice and in finding my true allies and supporters. I quickly learned to define my values and beliefs, and defend them by speaking the truth. I learned to set very clear boundaries rather than retreat to my age-old pattern of sacrificing my own happiness rather than stand up for myself. I defined what was non-negotiable for me going forward and took a stand, especially in relation to the importance of unconditional love (self and others) and support. It was like watching a perfect storm blow through my life, uprooting everything without substance, and then, after the winds had died, having only the strongest foundations remain, one of which was self-belief. The whole process taught me to never fear chaos, as it clears the way ahead.

I open my wardrobe and see the dress still hanging there, only now I look upon it from a place of calmness. My dreams of wedded bliss have not been lost; they have simply changed. Now my dream is not on the who, how, where, and when, but instead, it is simply on the desired end result of experiencing bliss. How, where, and when it happens … well, I have surrendered that completely to the universe. Meanwhile, the dress hanging in my wardrobe reminds me to never get lost in a dream so deeply that I lose touch with reality, while at the same time, it reminds me to never stop believing in love. Without force, it will come.

For now, I am grateful for the real-life Aanandha that I feel every day from the lessons I have learned. After all, what use was that time in my life if not for the incredible lessons learned? As Susan Hayward quotes in *A Guide for the Advanced Soul*, "Life is like a wild tiger. You can either lie down and let it lay its paw on you on your head, or sit on its back and ride it."

Full Moon Ritual

Under the healing power of the full moon,
the bearer of dreams, Celtic goddess Caer Ibormeith,
points the way to the labyrinth of your soul.

Close your eyes and see before you a labyrinth of stone
set in spiral, lit by candles, night flowers underfoot.
In the centre of the labyrinth stands Caer Ibormeith.
She beckons you to enter, to follow the spiral path
and unravel the truths from your dream state.
Step by step, follow her call into the labyrinth,
around and around; enter a peaceful and deep sleep
where secrets are revealed in your dreamtime.

May you close your eyes and dream tonight.
May your dreams be filled with colour and music,
softness and light, vibrancy and passion,
for in this dream state, you will return to the purity of the source.
May you see beyond any darkness that appears to surround you
in your dreams, for it is all but an illusion.

May you close your eyes and be renewed tonight.
May your body be filled with healing energy,
every cell experiencing regeneration and repair,
for in this dream state, your body is free from all damage.
May you accept peace in your body and feel freedom
from all physical ailments, for they are but illusions.

May you close your eyes and journey tonight.
May painful memories be diluted like
watercolour paints upon a canvas,
transformed to paint a new landscape,
where your heart may joyfully wander.
May you travel to beautiful places and experience
wonder like never before, for in your dreams,
restrictions are but illusions.

May you close your eyes
and awaken with love in your heart and
joy in your soul,
and may your blissful dreams be your waking reality.

Hope

When love takes over,
darkness turns to light,
sorrow turns to joy,
illness turns to healing,
loneliness turns to connection,
hunger turns to fulfillment.
Love entwines with hope,
hope embraces belief,
and faith is born.

Do you love to watch a thunderstorm roll in? There is something strangely mesmerising as a storm front approaches. We can feel the change in pressure, feel the energy change as towering cloud columns grow, flashes of lightning intensify, and then we wait for the thunderous crescendo. We find ourselves wishing for all it to continue as much as we want it to stop. Captivating battering winds and storm surges surprisingly draw people out from the safety of their homes to view and experience nature at her most powerful, as natural raw beauty combines with heightened senses and adrenaline, creating a combustible environment that can change for better or worse in a heartbeat.

One of the most enjoyable topics I studied at school was weather, especially extreme weather (in fact, it was the only class I enjoyed). I have always been drawn to tornadoes; maybe that has something to do with my love of the movie *The Wizard of Oz* from a young age, but for whatever reason, the fascination with this natural phenomenon has never left me to this day. I am in constant awe of the destructive power of the tornado, which can obliterate one home in a deadly waltz yet leave the neighbouring house completely untouched.

We weather all sorts of storms and turbulence in our daily lives, and most of those go completely unnoticed by others. Some of us may feel trapped in the grip of a tornado at this moment, where normality has been taken over by an unwelcome, uncontrollable force, and a path of destruction is being carved into what was previously an idyllic landscape. For those touched by death or terminal illness, that may well be their experience. For those experiencing divorce, family violence, the end of a relationship, illness, or unemployment, they may also feel like a tornado is ripping through their lives.

Strangely, it is not uncommon in such circumstances for so many bystanders and onlookers to feel completely helpless, just as if they were watching a storm in nature, captive but helpless and unable to offer any meaningful assistance. So often then, being held captive by a storm is a solitary journey, which increases the level of trauma experienced.

While chaos and destruction may feel all-consuming, while we may struggle to find shelter as the storm rages on around us and through us, there is always an opportunity for new growth when the wind dies and the dust settles. We may not see immediate opportunities, for with any loss, there is the natural process of grief to deal with, but we will ultimately see and experience growth because there has to be hope. We begin to see the beauty of things when we look at them for long enough in a different way, and after loss, we all hope to see and experience some beauty.

Elizabeth Kubler-Ross wrote in, *On Death and Dying*: "If you shield the mountain from the wind storms, you never see the beauty of the carvings."

There is strength in accepting, as the starting point, the aftermath of storms or tornadoes that may devastate our lives. With hope, wisdom, and grace, we can move forward. The pain of loss can be slowly replaced with the joyful memory of the gift of life and love. Destruction can slowly be replaced with the gift of growth and repair. Anger can slowly be replaced with the gift of energetic passion. When we see the beauty of things through eyes of love, we can rebuild lives and restore hope.

"Common experience teaches that, when great demands are made upon us, if only we fearlessly accept the challenge and confidently expend our strength, every danger or difficulty brings its own strength." J. A. Hadfield writes in *The Psychology of Power*.

Whatever storms may roll into our lives; we must hope better days lie ahead for us. For without hope, we may forever be consumed within the walls of a deadly tornado.

Sacred Blessing

May you be blessed with eternal love.
May you find true success measured not by your
accomplishments, achievements, or possessions,
but by the measure of love you share and by the measure of love
you are blessed with.
May you be blessed with the vision to see that which needs to be seen
so that your journey may always be guided in love.
May you forever have faith in yourself and others,
remembering we are all created from the same divine light.
May you be blessed with the knowledge you are part of
a universal family who
believe in you, care for you, love you, and support you.

You are a miracle of life.
Live with hope.
Live with love.
Live.

Embrace

We yearn to travel the world,
yet we are already travellers
of the universe,
moving to and fro in an
exquisite chariot made of love.

Whenever I struggle to get out of bed in the morning, I think of these words from *Soul Shifts* by Barbara De Angelis: "There are people who are going to die by the end of today. There are people who would give anything to have one more day with someone they love. There are people who would gladly take every day someone else decides doesn't count and add it to their life span. The truth is, every day is precious, and every day counts."

Shortly after I began volunteering in a palliative care setting, I experienced a day that proved to be precious beyond words. I held a dying woman's hands in mine and comforted her while she was lovingly and respectfully bathed, cleaned, and soothed by an incredible nurse. It was the most humbling and beautiful experience I have ever been witness to.

I thought it would be confronting to see a body ravaged by illness, but such a selfish thought had no place in the moment and was instantly dismissed. On the grand scale of things, there was no room for such an utterly useless concept of feeling challenged by the sight of a naked body. This was a human being, after all. My attention was instead focused on the beauty of the scene unravelling before me. There we were, three women, strangers to each other, coming together to care and be cared for. I was privileged to be a part of this act of unadulterated, unconditional love.

I am unsure if the sacred ritual of bathing another has perhaps become ingrained to those who perform such tasks on a daily basis, but the care delivered by this nurse showed no trace of being routine. I was completely left in awe of the woman who worked before me.

To see a human body at its most vulnerable and delicate state spoke a million words to me. There was nothing ugly, nothing shocking, nothing to see other than the beauty that is the human form. The body is the golden chariot that transports our soul through this wonderful life. It is an incredible miracle, capable of immense accomplishments, including creating new life, and yet we spend so much time hiding it away, consumed by what we see as failings when we look in the mirror.

We are obsessed by our appearance for too long in this life, at the expense of things that truly matter, and yet as if by some strange form of irony, at the end stage of life, the body is hidden in plain sight, obscured by the incredible beauty of the soul within. It is the soul that radiates and speaks volumes, without any words required. It is the soul that touches the hearts of others. The body simply functions, like it always has, until the end.

If we are living a life where we judge people by the chariot they are transported through this life in, including looking at ourselves in the mirror, then we are not seeing the exquisiteness of the soul within; and we are missing the point of our existence entirely.

Get on with life; get on with a meaningful life. Love all your lumps, bumps, curves, and dents. They are unique to you. Love your hair: your flat, frizzy, short, long, thinning, too-thick hair. Love your legs and arms: your cellulite, flappy bits, hairy bits, and dry bits. Love your too-small, too-close, too-big, going-blind eyes. Love your feet: your rough parts, ingrown nails, short fat dumpy toes. Love it all. Just love it, and get on with doing something more meaningful, rather than obsessing, preening, and criticising.

Love every bit of you while you live and breathe. Love every bit of you while you have the time and ability to enjoy the incredible experiences this physical chariot enables you to enjoy. Because just maybe, sooner than you expect, it will be time to hand it back.

Sacred Ritual from the Elemental Realm

The elemental realm offers you a beautiful gift under the influence of the sacred equinox. The flower faeries convey the blessing of sight into their realm and bestow joy and happiness upon you.

They offer you the gift of healing by guiding you on a beautiful journey of visualisation.

Create a sacred space, light some candles, and be still. Into a bowl of fresh clean water, place droplets of these essential oils:

- rose, signifying love and the heart chakra
- lavender, signifying intuition and the third eye chakra
- ylang ylang, signifying creativity and the sacral chakra
- chamomile, signifying confidence and the solar plexus chakra

Place your hands into the water and then remove them and rub your palms together three times. Holding both hands in front of your face, breathe deeply. Repeat the process, holding both hands before your face, heart, and closed eyes, breathing deeply.

Now dip your fingers into the fragrant water and anoint the pulse points of your body, located at your temples, throat, inside elbows, wrists, behind your knees, ankles, and the top of your feet. Do this ceremoniously and with love, respecting the over soul of the oils.

Sit in peace, relaxed and enveloped in the beautiful floral essences. Then see, sense, or visualise before you a large blank canvas. Visualise dipping one finger into the bowl of flower essences, then touch the canvas. See before you, delicate brush strokes begin to appear. Delicate elongated petals of the ylang ylang flower emerge, sunlight yellow in colour. Watch as the over soul of the flower creates beautiful images of its life.

Adding another drop of flower essence to the canvas, you see the pale-green bud of a rose appear. Watch as it opens to reveal a stunning pink bloom. Tendrils become visible; green budding tendrils full of growth and promise burst to spill vibrant pink blooms onto the canvas. The creation forming before your eyes conveys the life of the flowers that anoint your body and whose energy now blends with yours.

Place another drop of the flower essence onto the canvas and be delighted by the stunning carpet of white daisy-like chamomile flowers that take shape amidst the pink roses and sunlight-yellow ylang ylang flowers. The over soul of the chamomile graces the canvas with her beauty. Breathe deeply and revel in the delight that forms before you.

A final drop of flower essence is now added to the canvas, bringing to life the over soul of the lavender. Soft green stalks appear as if painted by the finest brush, then tiny, delicate purple flowers pile together, forming long buds bursting with fragrance and mesmerising colour.

Watch as the painting before you continues to form. What do you see? What has been created for you? Inhale deeply and be transported to wherever the flowers take you. Step into the image before you. Be healed by the flower essences as you journey. Have you entered a secret garden? Have you been transported to a faraway place? Are you relaxing in a beautiful garden? Spend time in this creation: seeing, feeling, sensing, inhaling, and healing.

When you are ready, raise your face towards the sky, as the beautiful healing flowers raise their faces to the sun. Breathing deeply, open your eyes and give thanks to the flower essences for sharing their sacred splendour and healing powers.

Create

Open your mouth,
but not before
you open your heart.

I have always had a bit of a secret love affair with velvet. My mother had a beautiful claret-coloured velvet skirt suit when I was young, but I could never understand why she wouldn't wear it. It had been a gift from my father, and I remember her saying that it was ugly. I personally thought it was the most beautiful thing I'd ever seen, and I would sneak into her room to look at it and touch it. In my early twenties, velvet became fashionable again, and I was so excited. Even more so, I was excited by the fact that I was working and could buy my very own velvet trouser suit. I wore it to death, of course, just to make up for lost time and before velvet went back out of fashion … which it did

I think my love of velvet is comparable to holding a flame for my father. I knew the claret velvet suit must have cost him lot of money. I hardly ever saw him because he worked all the time, and so I felt, even as a young child, that I appreciated all that the velvet suit represented, not to mention I saw it a sign of love, a gift from his heart. I was shocked to hear how much my mother disliked it, and I recall feeling a stab at my own heart as she mentioned to me that she did not care for it. It is my first memory of hearing words like that. As a result, I have always hated the thought of someone buying clothes for me, and throughout my entire life, I have asked people to never buy me clothes. No exceptions, not even for anything made of velvet. The sole reason for this is that I have never wanted to hurt someone by my dislike of something they took the loving time to choose for me.

The sight of a colleague in velvet pants recently brought my mind back to my mother's velvet suit. Her simple words spoken to me as a child had settled inside me and have shaped my thoughts to this very day. Words can have such a lasting effect on anyone, as we know. We have all said things during our lives and had no realisation of the impact they had, or perhaps we did and then instantly wanted to take them back … which is, of course, impossible. Every bad word uttered or written will leave its imprint. You may have been on the receiving end of many a harsh word at some point in your life, or maybe words were spoken that cut deep, like a knife. The effects of words can last a lifetime; some words can even steer some souls to take their own lives.

Rumi teaches us to refrain from speaking ill of anyone, ever. He goes so far as to say that we are obligated to hide the faults of others, by not speaking ill of them. When we let go of the "What's in it for me?" thought process, it is easier to think about our words before they leave our mouths. Learn to detach from our expected outcomes. It is better to be silent than to speak ill of another. Even better, we should say something from a place of love, or nothing at all. We need to learn to listen rather than just hear. Most of us hear what we think we want to hear and then respond, but we should stop and ask ourselves what people are really trying to say to us when they gossip. Are they feeling vulnerable or lonely themselves? What is really being said when people scream words of anger? Are they feeling threatened or powerless? From really listening, we can use our words to heal rather than escalate anger or prolong fear. If we find ourselves bombarded by people who continue to speak badly of others, who judge people and condemn them, we should ask them to stop, or if that is too harsh, we should stay quiet instead of being carried up in their storm. Soon enough, they will realise we won't be dragged into their drama.

Words are what shape us and the world around us, good and bad. Words can range from those as soft and nurturing as velvet to those which are corrosive as acid and all manner of in between, but they all come from our own mouths, and that means we have the choice to speak words of honey or speak words of vinegar. We should try to focus increasingly on our words every day, taking care to ensure they instil love into every situation.

"It is a Sufi teaching that one of the human being's greatest endowments is the power of the word. It is given to us as a token of the Creative Power that has been vested in every human being." Kabir Helminsk says in *Rumi on the Heart's Journey.*

The power of the word is far greater than we give thought to in our everyday lives. We think we are separate from the headlines we read and the news we hear, which is full of fear, but in reality, we may be doing more damage on an hourly basis with words falling carelessly from our very own mouths.

Sacred Blue Moon Mantra

Blue is the colour of the throat chakra, our centre for communication with others and with ourselves. Under a beautiful blue moon, take sacred time to open the throat chakra and bathe in the celestial pool of magnificent moon energy. It is the perfect time to be released from harmful cycles, as universal energies are amplified.

Visualise a beautiful moon glowing radiantly in the heavens.
Focus on the centre, the divine white light
surrounded by the blue of the moon, reflecting
deepest blue on the surface of the ocean.
Focus on the beautiful hues of blue, healing, calming.
Let the colour blue surround you.
Be consumed in all shades of blue that you can imagine.
Float in a sea of blue moonlight bliss.
Breathe in beautiful blue sparks of divine energy
until your entire body glows iridescent shades of blue.
Feel cleansed, calm, and deeply rested.
Then repeat the mantra until you are consumed in blue energy.

Throat Chakra Mantra

I speak loving words of truth.
I listen to my inner self, and I trust.
I communicate from my heart.
I am able to lovingly express myself.
I speak with love always.
Whenever my loving words falter, may I gracefully stop myself
and commence with words of love again.
I am willing to surrender old patterns and
words that hurt myself and others.
I am willing and able to speak from the heart
from this moment on.
I surrender in this sea of heavenly blue cast by this lunar beauty
and gratefully receive this healing ritual.
I feel gratitude for my spectacular life.

Compassion

Listen not to the words,
but take note of the actions.

Would you dare to take a walk in another person's shoes for one day? Would you be willing to become fully immersed in their struggles, fears, and challenges? Could we really consider a day without our current level of knowledge, life experience, community, emotional maturity, job, finances, home, wisdom, and self-awareness? Would we know where to begin or even what to begin, if all of those things we take for granted were wiped clean or, worse still, replaced by a lifetime of abuse, neglect, poverty, and helplessness? Looking from the outside in, so many people think they know they could do better, know they could turn their life around if they were in that position and know they could get out of a rut if they found themselves in one, but without understanding the complexities of the individual, this can be a very dispassionate viewpoint. Who are we to look upon another and judge their "failings" for having put themselves in a disadvantaged position? Are we so naïve? In reality, we know nothing other than what we choose to see with our blinkers on, from our place of security. As John and Lyn St Claire Thomas wrote in *Eyes of the Beholder*, "Truth does not change although your perception of it may vary or alter drastically." So what truths are we seeing if we are looking from a position of judgement, because that is ultimately what is going on?

Pity on the other hand, serves no one. There is a real differnce between feeling sorry for another while elevating oneself in the process, as opposed to being compassionate. It is compassion that is the key, the actual feeling of sorrow for another while being motivated to take real action to help without any motive other than to ease their suffering. Compassion is an act of pure love. It is something that costs nothing, and yet love can be so easily overlooked and replaced by judgement or disinterest. The phrase "made their own bed, so they can lay in it." was something that I heard often when growing up. To me, it was a phrase that embodied a washing of the hands. It meant that no help would be offered to someone, nor any sympathy given for someone who had made a bad choice and was suffering. Cruel words indeed that my conscience, in opposition to that way of thinking, throws up one of the very few Bible verses I can recall: "He that is without sin among you, let him first cast a stone at her." (John 8:7).

We are responsible for ourselves and for others because we are not separate from each other, as we would like to think. That doesn't mean we should try and save everyone from themselves. To begin with, it would be narcissistic to presume we knew every problem someone needed solved. We would be conceited to think we knew every correct answer to those problems. This doesn't mean that we should apply the "made their own bed, so they can lay in it." metaphor, either. But it does mean that love is needed. Love transforms every situation and should always be the first thing we think of in any situation. Injecting love into a thought, word, or action, before judgement, envy, jealousy, or disinterest takes hold, can only positively affect all concerned, including those who are in turn affected by the ripple that love creates.

In the book *The Prophet*, philosopher and writer Kahlil Gibran writes of love, "When love beckons to you, follow him. Though his ways are hard and steep. And when his wings enfold you, yield to him. Though the sword hidden among his pinions may wound you. And when he speaks to you, believe in him. Though his voice may shatter your dreams as the north wind lays waste the garden."

Once we have heard love call to us, and we have followed that calling, life seems to present more opportunities to us in which our loving practices can be shared. Just as we have been conditioned to keep our love separate from one person to another, just as we have been conditioned to judge on sight and blame others for their own suffering, we can become conditioned to the reality that true love knows no boundaries. True love is indeed the north wind, laying waste to the garden of preconceived ideas, beliefs, and conditioning.

"Man cannot discover new oceans until he has the courage to lose sight of the shore." (André Gide).

So dive. Dive into the deep, down and down where so many hearts and souls wait for the light of love: our love. Let it shine to guide them home to wholeness, for in return, our own hearts will expand and grow in ways we could never dream of.

Sacred Healing Blessing

Beloved, may you feel peace in your heart.
May your heart glow with radiant universal light.
May you experience life force in every cell of your being.
May you feel the power of life within you and through you.
May your mind be illuminated with good and loving thoughts
of yourself and of others.
May your mind be free of distortion.
May you fully experience the healing effects that a loving mind
can have on your body and this world.
May you be blessed with freedom from pain of the heart, mind, and body,
so as to honour the divine beauty of your soul.

With each in breath, peace now flows into your body.
With every out breath, love and compassion is imparted into the world.
The balance you feel with each breath is confirmation
of your acceptance of this healing gift of love.

Courage

It lies within us all.
It is the hunter in constant pursuit of the ego,
healer of trauma, and our protector.
It is our inner light.
Courage.

Driving along the expressway one morning, I was amused (for probably too long) by a large plastic lid, rolling between the lanes of traffic motoring along at 100 KPH, being buffeted and kept upright by the air flow of the cars. It just couldn't escape, and I thought it was quite funny. On and on it rolled with the relentless traffic. It was going at an amazing speed, rolling, rolling, jumping, and rolling, forever gathering momentum. Eventually, I drove past it and saw in my rearview mirror that it just kept going. It made me smile, and I sympathised with its plight, saying out loud, "Poor lid!" Hang on … it's a lid, a plastic lid.

As always, there was a message in the mundane. This plastic lid suddenly reminded me of how I had once been caught up in life and driven along for what felt like an eternity by the flow of other people. Kind of like being picked up by the momentum of the crowd at a tube station, and before you know it, you are on the tube, the doors have closed, and you're on your way to who-knows-where.

No matter how much I tried to get out of the way, the push and pull of others seemed to keep me trapped on a relentless path. Buffeted by thoughts, actions, words, assumptions, expectations, and fears, I went careening through much of my life on a road I did not want to be on. I then realised something: I hadn't been sympathising with the plastic lid; I had been empathising. I could see myself as the plastic lid: rolling, rolling, rolling.

We have all gone along with things in our lives for whatever the reason. For some people, that may mean peace and happiness, but if there is a voice inside, screaming, "This is not what I want." then something has to change, for everyone's sake.

Here is what I learned from my time as a plastic lid: Don't wait. There will never be a right time, and there will never be a right place. We may grow old and die, waiting for the stars to align, our ducks to be in a row, or our hero to arrive. There will always be one more excuse. Christmas is coming, it's so-and-so's birthday soon, holidays are here, the car needs fixing, I have a doctor's appointment, there are bills to pay, the kids have to finish school, dinner needs to be fixed, the house needs to be cleaned, once I lose ten pounds … and on and on and on it goes. Rolling, rolling, rolling.

Jump! Jump while we have the spirit, the thoughts, and the dreams. Don't become a plastic lid, stuck on the highway to hell, because by the time we come to a stop, we may be too worn out, too frayed, and too scared to pick ourselves back up again.

As James Roberts says in *The Nature of Personal Reality*, "You are given the gifts of the gods, you create your own reality according to your beliefs. Yours is the creative energy that makes your world. There are no limitations to the self except those you believe in."

We should believe in and follow our own desires instead of those created for us or dictated to us. We need to find our own voice, find our courage, and follow our heart's desires. We *can* make every day count, and we should thank every plastic lid we see on our travels, as they remind us to never roll to anyone's beat but our own.

Super Full Moon Warrior Goddess Ritual

Journey under the super full moon to a place where the warrior goddess is created. Call upon the elements, and draw on their power. Be brought to life, and harness the raw passion of the universe with this meditative ritual.

Walk barefoot along the earthy track stretched out before you.
Tall blond grasses weave either side, guiding
you and whispering their welcome.
Hear the roar of the ocean as you approach
the edge of a high clifftop.
Feel its power resonate deep within your chest.

The moon is high above you as you reach the edge.
Far beneath, high waves crash against ancient hard rock,
and in the water, dolphins circle … waiting, anticipating.
Feel the power of the wind, and inhale the salty ocean scent.

Silhouetted in the moonlight,
raise your hand to the east,
to where a volcano sits in the distance.
Watch as its glowing red liquid erupts and
flows at your command,
lighting tracks in the mountainside,
growing in strength and in speed towards the
passion and fire that now rests within you.

Raise your hand to the west, and command
towering storm clouds to form.
Watch as their power intensifies
and magnifies, as they speed towards the energy and strength
that now rests within you.

Standing on the precipice of this sacred spot,
you are a warrior goddess, abundant with strength and courage.
Call upon the elements that surround you.
With both arms raised to the indigo sky above,
call upon the wisdom of the ages,
and channel the elements into your being.

Thunder cracks, lightning flashes, waves crash.
Lava spouts and flows, winds blow fiercely,
and below, dolphins dance in delight
at this frenzy of energy and passion.

As the full moon reaches her peak
and all powers are amplified,
the sacred powers of the divine masculine and feminine,
Mother Earth and the universe
are directed to your outstretched arms, body, and soul,
where they take hold, and you are brought to your knees
in recognition of the power from which you are born.

Under this full moon,
you are blessed with the power of the universe;
you are blessed with raw elemental power.
You are blessed with humble awareness of the responsibility that is yours.
You are blessed with the gift of life and the passion of love.

You are the lava in full fiery flow.
You are the wind in destructive fury.
You are the sea in crashing strength.
You are the moon in rhythmic dance.
You are the power of nature.
You are the warrior goddess.

Release

You are always protected
and stronger than you
can ever imagine.
Stand tall, and draw upon the universal love that
never stops flowing to you and through you.

They say insanity is repeatedly doing the same thing, while expecting a different result. If that is true, then I have tangoed with insanity many a time, but thankfully, it has been a long time since insanity and I joined hands for a trip around the dance floor. That was, until I prodded an angry bear and was reminded that it's best to let sleeping dogs (bears) lie, and I parted ways with insanity for good.

Sometimes, we forget how far we have progressed, how much wisdom has been learned from experience after experience, and for just a second, we engage with ego, be it our own or someone else's. Old habits die hard, as they say, and we are always learning, but I knew better. I should have listened to my wisdom, and I must say that as soon as the bear roared, I knew that time had not healed it, time had not softened it, and I knew that the intuition I carelessly ignored had been spot on.

It's not easy to calm an angry bear down once it's on its back legs, but I knew this was my last tango with this particular bear as soon as I stepped to the edge of the dance floor. In fact, I had been praying for this bear's heart to be filled with love for the preceding month or so, praying that love would take hold. That compassionate action went a long way in me being able to remain at peace while the bear hurled criticism and judgement towards me.

It is almost impossible to be angry (ego) or scared (ego) when we step back and view a situation as an observer. So there I stood, at the edge of this imaginary dance floor, detached from the growling bear, lashing out and goading me to step in and take part. Detached, I reminded myself this was old wounds at play. I had forgiven this person previously. I had visualised them stripped of all their drama and saw only their inner light. There was nothing else to forgive. It had all gone before. This last tango was nothing more than a quick turn on the dance floor for old times' sake, and I found myself smiling as I thought of the insanity that was at play ... and then I was done.

Just when we think are free, we find ourselves reminded by the universe that there is even more freedom to be experienced. This last tango affirmed that

I was no longer affected in any shape or form by whatever could be said or done by this person because in being able to remain at peace when criticised, I felt divine confirmation of the enormous growth of inner confidence that I had experienced. It was confirmation that my foundational beliefs and values were strong, thus resentment and anger knew no place. This was an entirely new level of freedom. *Can it get any better?* I asked myself. Yes, was the intuitive response.

If we develop deep self-confidence and think compassionately of others, we will not only be able to remain at peace when criticised by others, we will also be able to cast off the shackles of the ego, which takes its form in defensiveness, resentment, fear, and anger. "Be afraid of nothing, you have within you – all wisdom, all power, all strength, all understanding." Eileen Caddy writes in *The Dawn of Change.*

Yes, we do indeed. I have danced my last tango with an imposing, roaring bear and have left insanity well and truly on the dance floor as the lights go out on that chapter of my life. Permanently.

Sacred Ritual for a New Beginning and a Wiser You

As a black moon rises, a new beginning and new cycle of life is heralded. It is a potent time to set new intentions and to call on universal energies to assist you on your sacred journey. Animal totems and sacred energies gather now to offer you great insight and help you reach your highest good.

White eagle soaring,
where will you show me today?
Where will you take me upon your back?
Soaring high above the treetops, with air beneath your wings,
all that needs to be seen can be,
and I am blessed with the gift of your sight.

Red salmon running,
where will you take me today?
Up rivers and running rapids I will journey with you,
with water rushing through your gills,
all that needs to be seen can be,
and I am blessed with the gift of your speed and stamina.

Brown bear roaming,
where shall we travel?
Across meadow and mountain, I will journey with you,
with soft earth beneath your paws,
all that needs to be seen can be,
and I am blessed with the gift of your strength and courage.

White spirit, all encompassing,
where have you brought me today,
in the form of sacred animals?
I have journeyed far and wide by land, air, and water
to reach this sacred gathering place.

Animal totems and elements combine
with the fire of alchemy, and
I am blessed with the powers of
dreams, communication, protection, and transformation
under this powerful black moon rising.
This gathering has forged great gifts
and blessed me with inner strength and wisdom.

Present

If you spend so much time looking behind you
to the past,
you may as well live like an owl,
forever in the darkness.

Can you recall a specific period in your life when you thought everything was just perfect, life was great, all was good? I'm sure you can; we all can. If that perfect time has now passed, just how often do you think of the good ol' days? Do you dream of having that time back and stepping into that moment? Are you currently caught between worlds, with one foot in the past and one foot in the future, standing in what feels like no-man's land?

If we are caught between worlds, we may feel incredibly stuck, unable to move forward, unable to move back, with the present just throwing chaos and conflict at us. Being caught between two worlds can feel like everything and everyone is working against us, blocking our way and every means of getting us back to that perfect moment in time.

Sometimes, when we are stuck between two worlds, we try so hard to change and control external environments in an attempt to relive the good ol' times that we lose our place in life. We feel a sense of abandonment, a sense of almost being orphaned, left to get on with it all, with no one really understanding what is going on underneath the surface. Sometimes, we don't even know what is going on under the surface ourselves; we just know there is something better to be had, something that feels familiar and good, some "thing" that is just out of our reach.

The song "Blue Bayou" has a beautiful chorus that tells of a desire to go back to a time and place where life is good: "If I could only see that familiar sunrise through sleepy eyes, how happy I'd be." I think we all have a memory that we could label as our own blue bayou, a place in time where life was sweet.

So what stops us from going back to the sweet spot and living it every day? Usually it's time, money, and responsibility that are the first things to stand in our way. But then there is the reality: That time no longer exists. The people have moved on and lives have changed. We have grown ourselves in years, wisdom, expectations, and our desires have changed. So where does that leave us? Surely, there is more to be had than just a memory?

Of course, there is because from our elevated position in life, we hold a bird's-eye view of all that has gone before us. We can now look back on that sweet spot of life and dissect it. What is it we really long for from that time? What elements of our blue bayou are we seeking to bring into the here-and-now? What made that time so special, great, or perfect? Was it the people, the place, the lover? No matter how big of a list we make, we will find one common denominator: us. We were right there in the middle of it, and here's the thing: What made it so great for us might never have been felt by anyone else because it was our experience. That means, what we are looking for now is still inside of us.

So when caught between two worlds, there really is only one thing to do: Bring both feet to the present, stand tall, and look inside to find our sweet spot again. It's always there, always has been, and always will be. Don't let life and all its magic blow on by in the search for your old blue bayou.

Angelic Connection

The angels wish to remind you of the infinite supply of love that is available to all. They wish to comfort and assist you to be present. By stepping onto the mountain path in this angelically guided visualisation, you will be calling for angelic guidance and assistance, which will in turn flow to you unreservedly. Step onto the mountain path, beautiful one.

The morning mist hangs like a veil,
shrouding the mountain path before you.
Not a sound can be heard in this still moment.
In this beautiful silent space, time has stopped.

A single water droplet suddenly falls upon your
forehead from above.
The dense mist clears before your eyes,
revealing an angelic creature.
She places both hands on her heart and
then extends them towards you.
You are filled with a sudden rush of white light from her heart to yours.

She steps forward and embraces you, gentle and kind.
She bends and rests her forehead against yours.
You are reminded of the place of pure love
from which you are born.
You are reminded of the endless light that rests within you.
No words are exchanged. No words are required.

She reminds you of your great insight.
She reminds you of your divine purpose.

Close your eyes and absorb the beautiful images
that flood your mind from this angelic creature.
Absorb the beautiful sensations that flood your body.
Breathe in universal wisdom.
Feel divine love emanate from her body and wrap around you.
Graciously receive all this angelic being offers you.
She is here to guide you to wholeness.

As gently as her forehead was placed against yours,
you feel it draw back.
"Open your eyes, beautiful one", she whispers.
When you do, the angel has gone,
and the mountainside is blanketed
with white blossoms as far as the eye can see.
Walk in purity, with your heart full of love and light,
with the blessings of all angels,
as time begins once more,
and you are present.

Maturity

Unwrap the swaddling.
Emerge from the cocoon.
Let all that you cling to
be replaced with a never-
ending blanket of stars.

Adventure makes the soul sing. It also drives passion and creativity, and there is nothing quite like embracing the unknown in order to shake everything up. I have found there is nothing quite as liberating as throwing off the security blanket and feeling the freshness that rushes in.

In 2004, I emigrated to the other side of the world, and in 2009, I took a massive leap to break free from a toxic relationship and make it on my own with my children. It was a heart-stopping period of my life. At times, I felt like my heart would explode in my chest from fear and my throat close up in panic, but those feelings gradually dissolved, and instead, I came to feel as if my heart would explode from sheer joy and freedom. Instead of feeling that my throat would close in panic, I finally found my voice and myself. Me, my voice, mine. My heart and soul learned how to sing; it has never stopped, and along the way, I fell in love with this beautiful country.

My children and I quickly became accustomed to the beach at the end of the road and the salty sting of the sea water on our sunburned skin. We have spent so many wonderful days there, soaking up the sunshine and trying to infuse our milky-white skin with some golden Australian colour. I fell instantly in love with the sea breeze, which still blows through my bedroom on hot summer nights and makes white curtains float in the air like gossamer wings. My heart and soul have long been soothed by the rolling waves, and I never fail to pull the freshness of the ocean deep into my lungs when it fills the air in a salty statement of being.

We have walked through haunting stringybark forests and hugged huge gum trees too fat to get our arms even halfway around their trunks. On country drives, we still open the windows to breathe in the intoxicating smell of burning wood, the same way burning log fires in neighbouring homes entice us in the crisp winter air.

We have stood on the top of volcanic rims, as if standing on top of the world, and found red dust as fine as talcum powder in our boots, socks, and undies after a day quad-biking in the dry bushland. But what I love most about this beautiful country is the stunning, wide indigo skies filled to bursting with never-ending starlight. Even on cloudy nights, we never fail to gaze towards the heavens, hoping to be blessed with the sight of peeking stars.

It is in moments such as these that my heart fills to bursting, as I look at the enormity of the universe above me and remember the enormity of the journey I embarked on all those years ago. It is in these moments that I give thanks for the sheer delights and pleasures that I have experienced, with my children by my side in this incredible land. I have long washed off the life that once held me, the life I clung to from a cocktail of obligation, ignorance, and fear. This growth has given me a blanket of stars to sleep under, as a replacement for the blanket of self-doubt and stagnation that once cocooned me. I feel that in shedding the old me, the one who bloomed on very rare occasions, if ever, I have matured to an evergreen in this wonderful sunburnt country.

"And the day came when the risk it took to remain tight in the bud was more painful that the risk it took to blossom." —Anais Nin.

Ancient Gaia Wisdom under the New Moon

Universal insight is offered to you under the new moon, as Mother Earth gazes towards the heavens while holding you to her breast and rocking you in her arms. Be honoured by this gift, for it will stir deep and ancient memories.

Light some candles and dip into a heavenly bath under the new moon. Infuse the water with one cup of milk powder, one cup of Epsom salts, and scattered petals or herbs of your choice. Relax, breathe, and float away with this heavenly ritual:

> At the heart of the mountain rests a sacred pool,
> which is home to an ancient tree.
> Follow the consectrated path before you
> down to the water's edge.
> The turquoise-blue pool appears to be lit from below
> with flecks of silver and gold sparkling and shining in the water.
>
> Dip your toes into the inviting water.
> Now gently immerse yourself and float effortlessly
> under the stars above.
> The warm water sparkles and shines as if moon
> dust has fallen from the heavens.
> Notice a pulsating glow, slowing intensifying around you.
> Now watch as your body begins to melt into the water.
>
> Your life force is being transformed before your eyes.
> You are merging with the water molecules.
> Every cell of your being is absorbed by the water molecules, and
> you are drawn up into the water system,
> taken up by the roots of a magnificent tree.

Feel yourself travel through the strong roots,
as this ancient beauty devours you.
Feel yourself pass through the branches and into
the very leaf structure of the tree.
You are giving life and receiving life in return.
Ancient wisdom is being transferred to your cellular memory.
Centuries of planetary insight is now yours.

Be drawn fully through the tree until you emerge
in the form of a thousand water droplets resting upon
smooth leaves, like freshly fallen raindrops.
Rest there and experience this incredible union.

Now feel the ancient tree contract, release,
and shake you from its embrace.

Like diamonds pouring from the night sky,
you fall from the leaves of the tree
into the beautiful turquoise waters
where you are returned to wholeness,
imbued with miracles,
saturated with wisdom
under the shining stars.

Dance

Close your eyes.
Let your feet be guided by angels.
Let spirit embrace you,
and dance to the beautiful music within your soul.

By the shores of Lake Wakatipu on the South Island of New Zealand, the air is filled with melodies so graceful, they can only be described as communication direct from the soul of an angel. Surrounded by soaring snow-topped mountains, blue skies, and glacial waters that rise and fall like a heart beating in the land-locked lake, a piano busker touches the hearts of many, unknowingly coaxing them to dance to the music of life, yet never saying a word.

I have been blessed to travel to this beautiful country, whose energy resonates with me in ways that have never been rivalled to this day. My heart sings from the first glimpses of the mountains upon arrival. The air is like nectar to my lungs, and my eyes just can't take in enough of the natural beauty that surrounds me. And when there just can't possibly be any more wonder and awe to be had, I find the piano busker, with melodies that have captured the essence of my being in this beautiful wild land, for they reflect the sound of my soul.

My grateful heart and life are filled with beautiful music. The melody is one of immense freedom, love, and gratitude, and as my eyes scan the incredible snow-topped mountain scenery, the lush green pastures, and blue glacial water, I realise I have never felt more at home with who I am in this very moment. I close my eyes to the music, and instantly, I am flying high on the wind, rising and falling, gliding effortlessly with only beautiful landscapes before me. Water glistens below me, and the only sound is the melody within me.

You see, there comes a time when the music of life just picks us up and carries us upon its tune. We may glide on music notes like a bird floating on a summer breeze, high above the world below. We may be hushed into dreamland by the tones of a sweet lullaby, or we may be flung full-throttle into new experiences, with an adrenalin heart-pumping beat, but we *must* let ourselves be carried by the music of life at some point. We *must* let our spirit soar and experience the exquisite tonal essence of life. We *must* give ourselves permission to live within the music; otherwise, it will circle around us, and although we will hear the notes, until we let them carry us, we will never feel the elegance of the energy as it vibrates within us on a particle level and resonates with our soul.

Only one thing stands in the way: permission. Grant yourself permission to follow your bliss. Grant yourself permission to follow your heart. Grant yourself permission to live a joyful life, free of conformity and free of constriction. Unwrap the blindfold of permission from your eyes. Cut the ties of permission from your wrists and ankles. Unshackle yourself from the restraints of permission that bind you and hold you prisoner. Delete the words "I can't" from your life. Because, yes, you *can*. Then sound the note that calls your soul to you and experience the music of life. Fall into the arms of your melody and be taken on a journey of freedom, love, joy, and simplicity. Let it carry you near or far, home or away ... just let it carry you.

A sacred blessing
to prepare for each
sunrise and sunset:

If you cannot see the light within yourself or another, it does not mean it
is not there. Be the light you wish to see. Be the beacon spirit wishes you
to be. In this dialogue with spirit, be blessed with unconditional love and
guidance, and then go light up the world:

I am blessed to see your face
and the sparkle in your eyes.
I am blessed to hold you close
and feel the warmth of your embrace.
I am blessed to listen to your words
and share in your memories.
I am so very blessed.

I am blessed to just be here,
in this moment, by your side.
I am blessed to spend priceless time
in your presence
and to see your face light up when I share a smile.
I am so very blessed.

Brought together at this time,
we can share love and feel love,
for the light in our hearts
connects and remembers
we are but one,
and we are blessed.

May you be blessed with love,
and may you experience joy in the
simple expressions of abundance that surround you every day.
May you be blessed with the knowledge
that you can create beauty with every person you meet
by sharing a smile, touch, or embrace,
for you are precious, and you are so very blessed.

Divine Guidance

When in need of wisdom,
close your eyes and be divinely guided to
the answers presented to you
on the following pages.

Restore

Spend as much time as you possibly can outdoors.
When we connect with nature, our energy becomes lighter,
and a sense of renewed vitality sweeps through us.
Never mind the weather.
Even five minutes each day,
breathing fresh air and experiencing nature,
will help to restore you.

Respect

Focus on the mouth. Be mindful of what passes
your lips, both outwards and inwards.
The lips are the gatekeepers of our sacred temple, the last
defender against unwise choices that deny us nourishment.
They are the last bastion of our thoughts
before words flow from our mouth.
Respect all that passes to and from your mouth.

Dare to Dream

Daydream, meditate, lose yourself in beautiful thoughts.
Cut out images from magazines.
Fashion a dream board or create a scrapbook,
bursting with whatever makes your soul sing.
When we dream, we create,
for everything is born from thought.
Everything.

Let Go

Sometimes, we try too hard.
Sometimes, we are so focused on obtaining a specific outcome
that we forget to see millions of other possibilities.
It is time for stepping back and observing.
Let spirit take the reins.
It is time to relinquish control
and be the observant passenger instead.

Transform

With a little tenderness,
we can change a block of hard, smelly Parmesan cheese
into a beautifully fluffy soufflé.
We have the gift to turn heaviness into lightness.
We also have the gift of sacred alchemy,
where we can transform any situation with love,
joy, and of course, tenderness.
Transform heaviness into lightness, this will have a lasting effect.

Second Chances Are Everywhere.

If your thoughts have been of lost opportunities with
someone, or something, to right some wrong,
or to try again after seeming failure or loss,
then conditions are ripe to have another go.
Only pride is standing in the way.
Whatever transpires will let you move on
to be free for other opportunities.

Let in Serenity

Serenity is knocking on your door,
while a new sense of fire and passion
stirs within.
Feel the stirring inside, but then pause,
as you may take action
that is not for your highest good if you burst ahead.
Allow serenity to wash over you and through you.
Surrender to its motives, as it will help you find balance.

Purify

Love and compassion are needed
in all situations you find yourself in.
This is not a time to be carrying dirt, talking dirt,
or wallowing in the mud.
Morning and evening, visualise stepping into a pool
where you bathe in the warm waters,
and your body and mind are cleansed each day.
Prepare for purity of heart.

Be Honest

Honesty is the best way to go,
but don't take that as a licence to offend others.
Honesty comes from within,
from looking firstly in the mirror.
Do you like what you see?
Everything you are has been created by you.
You cannot blame anyone or anything.
See the power in that realisation,
for it offers you creative carte blanche to write a better script.

Step into the Light

Whose shadow do you walk in, whose shadow do you live in?
There is a difference between being dependable and being a shadow.
Trust your intuition to step out of the shadow side of life.
By caring for yourself, you will make better use of
the time you spend on others.
You can be warm and thoughtful without giving half of yourself away.
Be kind and show understanding, but no more half-living.

Nourish

Nurture, nourish, nurture. Repeat.
Don't give up on yourself.
Take one day at a time, and focus your attention on *you*.
Take a break from any relationship with food,
drinks, people, places, activities
that are preventing you from healing.
Commit to the relationship of self.
This is a time to avoid carelessness
and seek expert help if need be.
But don't forget to add some humour along the way.

Abundance

Worries about finances do not serve you.
Instead, give all of your money worries
over to the universe and ask
for assistance in creating abundance.
Know that abundance comes in many forms,
and you may be rich in so many ways already.
You just have to open your eyes
and your heart to see.
Everything is coming together for you.
Ask and you shall receive.

Face Facts

There are times when you
do not believe in yourself.
You are challenged now to resolve this inner conflict
by seeing the positive in all situations.
Your desire for something new is really a desire to
face this challenge first and foremost.
Nothing will quench your thirst until you learn from this.
Success and growth are assured when you face the
problem rather than pretend there isn't one.

Awaken

Are you being seduced by the story you are telling yourself?
Remember that we are creators, and you hold
in front of you a blank canvas.
What paints will you choose? What brushes?
What colours will you choose?
Walk in nature and be inspired by the palette of life.
It is time to get a clearer picture of what you have been missing.

Clear House

Something inside is pushing you to move on.
Take care of unpaid bills, and tie up
matters that are distracting you.
Your desire for new opportunities will be realised
once you have cleared space in your mind and in your life.
For only by clearing distractions can you achieve
meaningful growth.
New opportunities will flow towards you when you, in turn,
take one step towards your dreams.

Softly Softly

You are in a phase of healing, part of which
requires you to forgive yourself.
The sadness you feel is linked to your past.
Know that you can and will move on from this.
Clear away everything that no longer serves your highest good.
Your strength lies in your independence
and ability to find a creative solution.
Like a sacred alchemist, transform your pain into insight.
Have faith, and move forward with confidence.

Trust

There comes a time when things must end.
Fear cannot be allowed to take the reins
at this time.
Know that you are divinely protected, and
have faith that with every ending
comes a new and bright beginning.

Shine

Cross over to the sunny side of the street,
where everyone you meet smiles and says hello,
where mornings are a gift,
and bedtimes promise sublime slumber.
Waste not one more second.
All you need is an open heart,
then welcome in a new day and a new life.

Be Positive

Where is your mind?
Are you dreaming big or are you doubting everything
and everyone, including yourself?
Shift your focus to remain positive.
Tell unwelcome worries to leave, now.
Find a fun song that is your instant switch to lighter thoughts.

Accept Help

Do you carry the weight of the world on your
shoulders because to ask for help
would seem like failure?
Let people in.
Ask for help, and see the wonderful
relationships that fill your world.

Notes

1. Charlotte Bronte, *Evening Solace* http://www.bartleby.com/291/117.html

2. Shakti Gawain, *Creative Visualisation: Use the power of your imagination to create what you want in your life.* 2008

3. Anne Sexton, *Admonitions to a Special Person.* https://www.poemhunter.com/poem/admonitions-to-a-special-person/

4. Charles F Stanley, *Charles Stanley's Handbook for Christian Living.* 2008

5. The Serenity Prayer, http://www.catholic.org/prayers/prayer.php?p=2176

6. Elizabeth Kubler-Ross, *On Death and Dying.* 2014

7. JA Hadfield quote, from Susan Hayward, *A Guide for the Advanced Soul.* 1984

8. Anais Nin quote, from Susan Hayward, *A Guide for the Advanced Soul.* 1984

9. Eileen Caddy, *The Dawn of Change.* 1997

10. Jane Roberts, *The Nature of Personal Reality.* 1994

11. Andre Gide quote, from Susan Hayward, *A guide for the Advanced Soul.* 1984

12. Kahlil Gibran, *The Prophet.* 1991

13. John and Lyn St Claire Thomas, *Eyes of the Beholder.* 1982

14. Kabir Helminsk, *Rumi of the Heart's Journey.* 2010

15. Barbara De Angelis, *Soul Shifts* 2015

The music of the Piano Busker can be found at http://evolvingrhythms.com/

Printed in the United States
By Bookmasters